The Memoirs of an Ambassador; a Contribution to the Political History of Modern Times

THE MEMOIRS OF
AN AMBASSADOR

.

THE MEMOIRS OF AN AMBASSADOR

A CONTRIBUTION TO THE POLITICAL HISTORY OF MODERN TIMES

By FREIHERR VON SCHOEN,

former Secretary of State for Foreign Affairs and Ambassador

TRANSLATED BY CONSTANCE VESEY

LONDON: GEORGE ALLEN & UNWIN, LTD.
RUSKIN HOUSE, 40 MUSEUM STREET, W.C.1

First published in 1922

PREFACE

\

THE following statements are chiefly based on short notes, which were made immediately or soon after the events. They make no claim to be a history of the periods dealt with, their object is far more to throw light on a few details which still need some explanation. At the same time it has been necessary, for the sake of continuity, to relate much that is well known. Their publication has been delayed, partly in order to give precedence to those who had statements of more importance to make, and partly because it seemed better not to contribute anything further towards the elucidation of vexed questions which are still disputed, until the excitement should have subsided sufficiently to enable people to form a dispassionate opinion.

THE AUTHOR

BERCHTESGADEN.
In the spring of 1921.

CONTENTS

The Memoirs of an Ambassador

I

MINISTER IN COPENHAGEN

I HAD no thought of a diplomatic career when the question "What will you be?" was put to me. My idea was to devote myself to agriculture. This plan was knocked on the head by the outbreak of the Franco-Prussian War. I joined the Darmstadt *Chevauxlegers,* later on the Body Dragoons, as a volunteer, went through the campaign, became an officer and remained with the Colours. My being attached to the Embassy in Madrid decided my career. The insight thus gained into a wider and more important world than the one to be seen from the barrack-yard and parade-ground made a great impression on me; and at the end of my time in Madrid, when I was confronted with the question whether I would join the diplomatic service, I found no difficulty in deciding. After being employed at the Foreign Office, and at various Legations, I was appointed Councillor of Embassy in Paris, a position which became of great importance, both because I held it for an unusually long time, and because my Chief, Count (afterwards Prince) Münster, left the conduct of affairs very much in my hands.

My appointment to be Minister in Copenhagen early in 1900 gave me a more independent sphere of activity. It is true that this independence was restricted, for it is the essence of the diplomatic service, particularly in the form given it by Prince Bismarck, that the representatives in foreign countries must act strictly within the limits of their general or special instructions, and not as they may think fit. Still, the fact that I received no directions, beyond the conventional instructions to maintain good relations, indicated in my credentials, gave me a certain amount of latitude. I was left to gather the policy to pursue from historical precedent and tradition.

Our relations with Denmark were not altogether satisfactory. They were still influenced by the events of 1864, and did not extend much beyond a courteous but cool attitude in official intercourse. The two peoples came comparatively little in contact, and at times their attitude towards one another was churlish and even hostile. The state of affairs on the Schlesvig-Danish frontier, the obstinate resistance to Prussian rule, which was encouraged both openly and secretly from Denmark, was a fruitful source of friction and unpleasantness, and a fundamental obstacle in the way of better relations. In addition to this the Danes thoroughly distrusted us. We were regarded as the wicked, powerful neighbour, to whom it might occur some fine day to lay violent hands on weak Denmark, an eventuality which must be provided against as

far as possible by military and diplomatic precautionary measures. Although this suspicion was
very much due to sedulous prompting from outside, it must be admitted that it was encouraged
by the attitude of individual German circles, which
were bent on extension of power, and boasted of
Germany's military strength. Little or nothing was
done in responsible German quarters to counteract
this unfortunate state of affairs, or, at all events,
nothing likely to be of any use. It was thought
unnecessary to attach any great weight to our
relations with our smaller neighbours ; they were
hardly taken into political consideration at all, and
it was left to the local authorities in the country
to deal with the uncomfortable state of affairs on
the frontier as they thought best.

I considered it my duty to do all I could
to bring about an improvement in the relations
between us and our northern neighbour, not
only in accordance with my view of the
general obligations of diplomacy, but because
I recognised the value of being on good
terms with a country which held a position of
importance as mistress of the water highways, and
with which we were associated both by family
ties and an interchange of intellectual ideas and
material goods which was mutually advantageous.
That I achieved this comparatively quickly was
mainly thanks to the change of feeling in Denmark
which brought the Liberals into office instead of
the Conservatives, who were on the whole unfriendly to Germany.

The programme of the Liberal Party was the
maintenance of the strictest neutrality in all foreign

political matters ; they would have nothing to do with military efforts which had no prospect of success, and they more or less openly and emphatically pointed to the establishment of better relations with Germany as a goal worth aiming at.   The beneficial effect of this change became evident.   The attitude towards us in official circles became less prejudiced and more cordial, the Press was more friendly, less encouragement was given to the contumacy of the Danish inhabitants of Schleswig, and Germans visiting Denmark, or resident there, were not so often given the cold shoulder.

As this friendly policy was only making slow and tentative progress, it seemed advisable to further it at the right moment, and in such a way as to encourage without appearing to urge it.   In this sense a revival of the intercourse between the Courts of Copenhagen and Berlin, which had somewhat flagged, might be useful, for, in spite of a leaning towards democracy, the spirit of the Danish nation was strongly monarchical. A suggestion that the Crown Prince Frederick might like to take the opportunity of one of his regular journeys to other countries to visit the Court of Berlin, where he could be sure of a friendly reception, fell on good ground.   The visit soon took place, and was a great success in every way.   The Crown Prince returned with the pleasantest impressions, and made a point of letting this be known far and wide.   This was an important step in the desired direction ;   and the feeling between Denmark and Germany became obviously more cordial, which was very satisfactory.   With a view to establishing the cordiality still more firmly I took advantage of a Court entertainment in Berlin, with the Chancellor's authority, to urge the Kaiser to pay a visit to Copenhagen. The Kaiser readily fell in with the suggestion, and proposed April 4th, King Christian's birthday, for the visit, although I pointed out that the King's son-in-law, the Duke of Cumberland, with whom we were not on any terms at that time, was generally at the Court of Copenhagen with his family just then. The Kaiser took no exception to this, but unfortunately the Duke could not bring himself to meet the Kaiser, and avoided the meeting by leaving before his arrival, making the illness of one of his sons, who had been left at Gmünden, the excuse. I should have had no difficulty in preventing his going if I had been authorised to enter into the necessary *pourparlers*, but Berlin held firmly to the view that it was politically inadvisable for the Kaiser to have anything to do with the head of the house of Guelph. Later on the Kaiser confided to me that he would have been glad to meet the family, as the idea of marrying the Crown Prince to one of the Duke's charming daughters had occurred to him, and he also thought that a reconciliation with the house of Guelph would be a good thing from a political point of view.

In spite of this *contretemps*, the Kaiser's visit to Copenhagen went off very well, so much so that it was prolonged from four to five days at King Christian's wish. His reception by the general public was very different to that accorded him on the occasion of his first visit, fourteen years earlier. The people of Copenhagen were agreeably surprised at seeing a man whose manner was attractive and genial, who greeted the old King with filial deference, smiled in a friendly way at the populace, and devoted himself to sight-seeing during his stay, like a simple tourist, instead of the scowling War Lord artists and writers were so fond of depicting. It was a source of special satisfaction that the Kaiser should have paid a visit to the Town Hall, the *sanctum sanctorum* of a dignified *bourgeoisie,* and that he displayed no interest in military matters. This was all the more welcome to the Danes, who were opposed to any kind of militarism, since the modest conditions did not allow of a brilliant military pageant. The feeling was, in short, so cordial that an eminent citizen of the capital told me that, if the Kaiser would stay another day, the people, generally so difficult to rouse, would unharness the horses and draw the carriage themselves in their enthusiasm.

The visit made the pleasantest possible impression on the Royal family, and called forth repeated assurances on the part of the Monarchs that they would adhere loyally to the renewed relations of friendly confidence, and act as the nation's forerunners in the path of better understanding, on which they had made such a happy start. For the rest, political matters were very little discussed ; neither side proposed special agreements : it was tacitly agreed that the fact of the Kaiser's visit, and its success, would in itself have an excellent influence in the direction mutually desired. Mention must be made of the fact that the Kaiser's engaging manner made a lasting impression in his favour both on the

King's daughters, the Empress Dowager of Russia and Queen Alexandra of England, and on Prince Waldemar's French wife, Royal ladies who were all three credited with having occasionally played not unimportant parts in political matters, and in a sense hostile to Germany. After the visit there were no apparent signs of untoward feminine influence having asserted itself.

A second shorter visit the Kaiser paid to Copenhagen, in the summer of 1905, also had a good effect, principally because he disposed of the suspicion that he was opposed, in the interest of his own dynasty, to a Danish Prince being elected to the throne of the new Kingdom of Norway, after the separation from Sweden. I had already assured Danish statesmen that the Kaiser had no thought of interfering in any way in the question of the Norwegian throne, but the Danish uncertainty continued to receive fresh encouragement from England, until finally the Kaiser himself put an end to the nervous tension by saying to Prince Carl, the future King Haakon, by way of greeting, that he would be the first to visit him in Christiana.

It was on the occasion of this visit that the Kaiser, who had already spoken of the possibility of my being appointed Ambassador to St. Petersburg, informed me that, at a meeting with the Tsar at Björko, he had obtained his willing consent to a treaty of alliance, which Russia was to try to induce France to join, thus reviving an idea which had already been considered by Prince Bismarck. It was a very ambitious scheme, whose realisation would have secured the peace of Europe, but which was frustrated, as can readily be understood, by the disinclination of the French Government to enter into an agreement which would mean renunciation of any prospect of recovering Alsace-Lorraine. France rejected the suggestion at once, and in view of the weak and vacillating character of the Tsar, who, it is well known, could not hold out against the military pressure at a critical time later on, and preserve peace as he wished to do, it was not very difficult for Count Lamsdorff, the Russian Minister for Foreign Affairs, to refuse to pursue the matter any further, on the ground that the agreement had been reached without having been considered by the Cabinet, and without any reference to him. It had merely been discussed in the presence of the Minister of Marine, who was not competent to deal with it.

A satisfactory result of the events which brought about the revulsion of feeling was that, apart from the general improvement in the Germano-Danish relations, Germanism acquired a more independent and less unworthy position in Denmark. Hitherto, the Germans resident there had been obliged to adopt a very unobtrusive and submissive attitude. Efforts to hold gatherings, to start works of general utility, or to celebrate patriotic festivals, had made but very poor headway. The Minister had only succeeded with difficulty in collecting a few guests for his dinner in honour of the Kaiser's birthday. It seemed to me an imperative duty to put an end to this humiliating state of affairs, to profit by the more favourable circumstances to rouse the pride of my fellow countrymen, to promote the formation of associations, to establish institutions of general utility, and hold patriotic celebrations, and I had the satisfaction of finding that a great many Germans readily responded to the appeal, that works and organisations were started on a firm basis which did honour to the German name, and won respect for German purpose and ability, everywhere.

Although the predominant feeling was one of relief, the change in Denmark did not meet with unanimous approval in Germany. Satisfaction was felt in responsible quarters at a point having at last been reached, beyond which the path promised to be less stony than hitherto. A future seemed to be opening up, in which much that had been left undone in less favourable days might be done, and many difficulties might be adjusted. Public opinion was for the most part inclined to approve of the more amicable state of affairs in Denmark, believing that it was not merely a passing phase, but promised to be permanent, and that its value might be very much enhanced by further careful develop-ment. On the other hand, in extreme national-istic circles, both doubt and suspicion were felt, and fault was even found, particularly by those who thought the attitude of the Danish population in North Schlesvig justified this. The change in Denmark was noted, but it was thought right to utter a warning against over confidence in a substantially better future, and the Government was implored not to accede to the demands the Danes would be certain to make for milder measures in our frontier districts—*timeo Danaos et dona ferentes.*

The fact that my name was mentioned in connection with the improvement in the relations, which had been obvious during the Kaiser's visits, led to an idea that I advocated far too much compromise. This prejudice, which was founded less on facts than on pure supposition, and which I had no opportunity of dispelling, grew rapidly as time went on, and increased to such an extent when I was appointed Foreign Secretary that it became a sort of article of faith. People were so obsessed with this mistaken view that they chose to hold me responsible for the " Optants' Children " treaty, concluded in 1907, and for its consequences, regardless of the fact that I had nothing whatever to do with it. This would have been obvious to anyone who made the smallest inquiry into the circumstances, as I was neither Minister in Copenhagen nor Foreign Secretary in Berlin at the time of the negotiations, but Ambassador in St. Petersburg. An explanation I chanced to have later on with the leader of German opposition in Northern Schlesvig to Danish machinations gave me an instructive insight into the way in which political warfare is sometimes carried on. He had to admit that the belief which had for many years held me responsible for the conciliatory policy, which found expression in the " Optants' " treaty, was mistaken. The people, he thought, did not always know exactly when changes in office took place. This experience very much shook my opinion of the absolute objectivity of political warfare.

It was while I was Minister in Copenhagen that I had to accompany the Kaiser several times on his travels, as representative of the

Foreign Office, once on a short shooting expedition through Silesia, another time on the Mediterranean trip which took us to Tangier among other places. On the first of these opportunities I had of coming into closer contact with the Kaiser, he explained, having just received unsatisfactory news, how things might be if the pressure exerted by our opponents should become so marked as to compel Germany to defend herself against attacks from more than one quarter. Then Frederick the Great would be remembered, the *Furor Teutonicus* would break up the ring with irresistible force, the German armies would sweep through France like a hurricane, and after her speedy defeat would turn against Russia, whose preparations to fight would only be going on slowly, and would make very short work of her too. The Kaiser's opinion of England was that she would merely look on at first, and that the great struggle would be over before she had decided which side to take. So even then he was apprehensive of a great war.

As far as the Mediterranean trip is concerned, the proposed visit to Tangier was no longer a secret. It was often openly discussed, and more or less plainly spoken of as a serious warning to France, on account of the high hand she was taking in Morocco. It was also whispered that the Kaiser had only reluctantly agreed to such an unusual demonstration. As a matter of fact, I noticed in the course of the voyage that he was not looking forward to the Tangier adventure without some misgiving. He told me himself that he had not intended to let the trip assume the character of an important political demonstration; he had only wanted to give his numerous guests a passing glimpse of genuine Mussulman life, and thought of remaining on board himself at Tangier, as the East was not new to him'. But the Chancellor, presumably influenced by Herr von Holstein, had so firmly insisted on the political side of the visit being accentuated, that, true to the constitutional principle, he had finally given way.

In addition to his doubts as to the political wisdom' of the undertaking, the Kaiser was very much concerned because he had been told in Lisbon that the streets were too narrow to drive through, and that he was consequently expected to ride a horse to which he was not accustomed from the harbour to the Legation on the far side of the town. He had also heard that in case of a fresh wind blowing from the east it might be difficult, if not impossible, to land, for lack of a sheltered harbour. Now and then the Kaiser seemed inclined to back out of the promise he had given the Chancellor, on the ground that he had not known of these difficulties beforehand. His vacillation placed me in rather an awkward position : on the one hand I was personally convinced of the political and other objections to the undertaking, and on the other it was not only my duty, as the representative of the Foreign Office, not to allow the Kaiser to waver, but special stress had been laid on the duty. It was made easier for me by the presence of Count Tattenbach, the Minister in Lisbon, who had been in Morocco before going there, and had fought diplomatic battles against French presumption. He was a firm advocate of the Tangier adventure, and was accompanying the Kaiser to Morocco both as being familiar with the matter in hand and with the place. For my part I thought it best to leave the God Æolus to decide whether he would favour the enterprise or not.

When we arrived at the Tangier roadstead, sure enough a stiff east wind was blowing, so that landing in boats was out of the question. The Kaiser decided to wait for better weather, or to go to Gibraltar, if necessary, and come back from there. In the meantime the chargé d'affaires, Kuhlmann, succeeded in reaching the *Hamburg* in a sailing boat with the pilot, and getting on board by means of the rope-ladder —the sea was too rough for the steps to be used—covered with spray, and in the full uniform of the Bamberg Uhlans. The senior Captain of the French cruisers anchored in the roadstead also arrived on board to pay his respects to the Kaiser, who drew him into a long conversation about the weather. When the wind had fallen a little, General von Scholl, an aide-de-camp, was told to try to land and find out for certain whether there was any possibility of getting to the Legation. When the General returned and reported that there was no great difficulty in landing, if one did not mind getting wet, that the horse provided for the Kaiser was excellent, and that in the town all the world was awaiting the Kaiser in feverish excitement, the landing was decided on and accomplished without any trouble.

According to the papers the Kaiser made

speeches to the Sultan's aged uncle, and the representatives of the German colony who received His Majesty on shore, in which special stress was laid on the Sultan's independence and equality of right. The truth is that the Kaiser did not make any formal speeches, he merely replied to the addresses of welcome in a conversational strain, although indeed the purport of what he said was as stated.

We were within an ace of being prevented from carrying out the remainder of the programme, by the white Arab horse the Kaiser was to ride becoming restive at the unaccustomed sight of the helmet, and refusing to let him mount. The animal was reduced to obedience, however, and, followed by an escort of about twenty persons, all on horseback, the Kaiser rode into the town, where the narrow streets, filled with jubilantly noisy crowds, only allowed of a slow progress.

The flat roofs of all the houses were also packed with Moorish, Christian, and Jewish women, who hailed the Kaiser in a variety of keys, and scattered flowers. At last the cortège reached the Soko, the open space in front of the Legation garden. It was a seething mass of people, who displayed their enthusiasm by rending the air with deafening shouts, and shooting wildly in every direction. A military band sent by the Sultan, which vainly tried to drown the uproar made by the people, added to the confusion. The horse became so restive that I asked a French officer who seemed to be in command, whether he could not put a stop to the firing. He replied gloomily that he had some influence over the handful of regular troops which had been entrusted to him for training, but none whatever over the half savage Kabyles.

The Kaiser had an exhaustive conversation in the Legation with the Sultan's uncle, when he again promised to support the Sultan's claim to independence, and received other Moorish guests, as well as the Ministers of foreign countries. I now approached the Kaiser, pointing out that a historical event of an importance which could not yet be estimated had taken place, and urged his ordering a return to the ship. I was afraid that the longer the tension lasted, the more easily the excitement of the populace might lead to unpleasant incidents, and I also feared that, if the wind got up again, we might not be able to embark, and that the Kaiser would be detained in a Moorish town which was not controlled by any strong authority. Fortunately, we managed to get on board without any misadventure. It was only some days later, when the Kaiser first heard in Naples of the tremendous sensation his visit to Tangier had made in the world, that he seemed to become fully aware of its great political importance. Although he did not say so, my impression was that he looked back on the event with a feeling that it would have been better to have adhered to his original opposition to it.

Compared with Tangier, the rest of the voyage, which included visits to Corfu and places in Italy, as well as to Lisbon and Gibraltar, was of little political importance. A slightly discordant note was struck on the first day of our prolonged stay in Lisbon, by the Kaiser having replied in German to the French after-dinner speech made by King Carlos. This was received by the Portuguese with icy frigidity. King Carlos had not discussed the toasts which were to be exchanged, although he was alone with the Kaiser for hours in the State carriage in which the latter made his formal entry, and our Ambassador had also omitted to find out privately what the King intended saying, as is customary. Consequently the Kaiser had to reply on the spur of the moment. He may also have been feeling annoyed at a Portuguese wireless station having refused to accept a German telegram to the Empress, shortly before his arrival. I succeeded in persuading the Kaiser to make a hastily composed speech in French the next day at an entertainment given by the Geographical Society, an institution of which the Portuguese are very proud. He spoke of the deeds accomplished by great Portuguese navigators, and of Portugal and Germany's colonial achievements, and the coolness then changed to southern warmth and enthusiasm. The remainder of our stay in Lisbon passed off quite harmoniously.

After Tangier we paid a short visit to Gibraltar, where the English Governor—Sir George White, the defender of Ladysmith in the Boer War—entertained the Kaiser most courteously and graciously. The Kaiser was immensely gratified by his reception, and it was evident that, in spite of his political differences with the English, he was very much inclined to be attracted by the charms of English hospitality.

Another place we stopped at was the Spanish port, Port Mahon, where the General in command was deputed by the King of Spain to receive the Kaiser. Some embarrassment was caused by the fact that the General could speak no language but his own, so that I had to come to the rescue as interpreter with my somewhat rusty Spanish.

A meeting with the King of Italy, and three days the Monarchs spent together at Naples, when they saw more of one another than on previous occasions, was considered to have contributed to strengthen the idea of the Triple Alliance. But to have assumed that this fresh meeting between the Monarchs established relations of absolute con- fidence between us and our Italian allies would have been attaching too much importance to the event. This was another instance which showed that, as far as the relations between peoples are concerned, meetings between heads of States are usually of more apparent than real constructive importance. For that matter there was no special political object underlying this, any more than the Kaiser's visit to Italy the year before. He went for change and rest, and to make acquaintance with beautiful and interesting places. What particularly interested him from a historical and artistic point of view were the architectural remains dating from the Hohenstaufen period in Sicily and Apulia. The hints here and there in the foreign Press, that the Kaiser's visits to Italy were prompted by a vast scheme he had in mind for the restoration of the Holy Roman Empire, were merely the product of overwrought imagination.

The visit to Corfu was essentially of a friendly nature. As ill-luck would have it, neither King George nor any other member of the Royal family was there to welcome the Kaiser. King George had, with extreme courtesy, started to meet him in his yacht, but had gone south of the island, whilst the *Hohenzollern* arrived from the north, a game of hide and seek which the monarchs treated as a joke. His stay in the island, which was looking beautiful in its perfect spring garb, made such a happy impression on the Kaiser that he decided to acquire the Achilleon.

At the end of the Mediterranean voyage, the Kaiser told me that he had willingly agreed to the Imperial Chancellor's proposal to send me as Ambassador to St. Petersburg, but that it would be some little time before the post fell vacant. Count Alvensleben seemed to be thinking of resigning, but he had not yet officially notified his intention of doing so. Eventually the change was made towards the end of the year.

II

AMBASSADOR IN ST. PETERSBURG

WHAT really decided the question of my appointment to be Ambassador in St. Petersburg was, as the Kaiser and the Chancellor told me, that in addition to their appreciation of what I had done hitherto, they thought the fulfilment of my duties in a matter of great importance, that of personal influence in the highest quarter, ought to be very much facilitated by my already having made the Tsar's personal acquaintance. The fact of my being a Hessian, and having been Chamberlain in Coburg for a time, had given me frequent opportunities of meeting their Russian Majesties informally, and the assumption that I should be welcome at the Russian Court, as the Kaiser's representative, was therefore warranted. Besides this the Kaiser had written to tell the Tsar of the decision, at the same time expressing a hope that an old acquaintance would be specially welcome, and the answer had been friendly. The Grand Duke of Hesse had also written a few lines recommending me to his sister.

When I took over the post, towards the end of 1905, the conditions in Russia were still far from normal. It is true that, generally speaking, the revolution had been put down, but the fire often flared up dangerously in the capital and in the country. I had immediate proof of the uncertainty which was still very prevalent, on reaching the frontier station, Wirballen, where I was received by Colonel Massejedov, the police commandant. He accompanied me to the saloon carriage which had been prepared for me, and wished me a safe journey, adding that there were rumours current of impending revolutionary attacks on the railway bridges. He had not yet been able to ascertain how far there was any truth in the reports, still less to take any precautionary measures. I accomplished the journey, however, without any misadventure, and arrived safe and sound in St. Petersburg on January 1, 1906.

The expectation that I should meet with a cordial reception at Tsarkoe-Selo was amply fulfilled. During a temporary pause in the stiff ceremonial customary at first audiences, the Tsar and Tsarina received me on terms of intimacy. The conversation lingered long over old and happy recollections, and ended by the Tsar inviting me to come and see him informally if ever there were anything I wanted done, or I had anything on my mind. He said he would be glad to see me often. The Tsar kept this kind promise, although he naturally avoided showing any marked preference for the German representative.

Our relations with Russia at that time were as good as it was possible for them to be under the existing circumstances. It is true that they were still clouded by the fact of the Franco-Russian alliance, but as soon as the influx of French money had done its duty, the Russians had treated the alliance with a certain coolness. This coolness increased considerably as a result of the extremely cautious attitude adopted by France during the Russo-Japanese War, an attitude which was hardly that of an ally. On the other hand our not only loyal, but very, benevolent, and also disinterested neutrality was duly noted in Russia, and gratefully acknowledged. Both the Tsar and Count Lamsdorff, the Foreign Minister, took the first opportunity of telling me that our friendly attitude would not be forgotten. The Tsar said nothing about the relations with France beyond a few words of little more than a general nature, which did not, however, show any great enthusiasm. Count Lamsdorff went farther and was more outspoken. He said France's attitude during the war had been a source of great disappointment and annoyance in Russia. In so far as the alliance depended on national feeling, it had been very much weakened. But it was advisable, in fact necessary, to maintain it, in order to hold restless France in check—" *pour mater la France révolutionnaire* "—in the interest of European peace. Russian policy recognised this. From this point of view a continuance of the alliance could not menace us in any way, rather the contrary. He personally—and the Kaiser too —had no affection at all for France, but they were aware that foreign policy must be dictated by carefully weighed considerations, not by feelings. By not renewing the so-called Reinsurance treaty, we had done away with a powerful support of the very satisfactory position existing at the time, and Russia had been almost obliged to enter into a similar understanding elsewhere. The Minister only spoke with constraint and reserve of the Björkö agreement, which had since been repudiated. It was obvious that France could not be expected to enter the proposed alliance, although the idea underlying it was of course most excellent. He had been certain, directly he heard of it, that no effort in that direction would be of any use. It was unfortunate that he, the responsible Minister, had not been asked to come to Bjorkö; he would have uttered a warning against exaggerated hopes, and have prevented the monarchs from signing an agreement which it seemed impossible to carry out.

What the Minister said as to this was not at all a surprise, as we already knew that he had done nothing to induce France to agree to the desired alliance. He had confined himself to acquainting Russia's allies with what had taken place at Bjorko, and had promptly received the reply " *non possumus* " from the French. The position was, therefore, that those responsible for Russian policy had not thought fit to do anything to bridge over the existing differences between us and France, and put an end to a source of European discord, and had thus adopted an attitude which could only be understood in France as sanctioning the existing state of affairs. Besides this, the incident was instructive, for it showed that the Tsar's word was not as inviolable, and his power not so great, as was generally believed in Germany. If what had occurred had been widely known, which was fortunately not the case, it would have caused no little uneasiness, and capital would have been made out of it by representing it as an abortive German attempt to shake European policy to its foundations. But an undesirable impression was made, even in the minds of the few initiated, which cast a slight shadow over Russo-German official relations.

The shadow would have been darker but for the fact that the relations were furthered in other ways. In addition to our attitude during the Russo-Japanese War, our attitude at the time of the Russian revolution was also appreciated in Russian Government quarters, even though there was some inclination to look on it as a matter of course, less a mark of friendship than a necessity. The strict neutrality we had observed towards domestic events in Russia, as previously towards foreign events, gave satisfaction chiefly because this attitude expressed confidence that the existing Russian Government would succeed in tiding over the crisis without outside help. Our domestic political life was so essentially Conservative that it practically guaranteed our doing all that could be desired to check any attempts that might be made in Germany to back up the Russian revolutionary movement. But the fact that our Liberal Press observed great moderation was taken in very good part, whereas the opinions publicly expressed in France and England often roused bitter indignation.

It is characteristic of the Russian mentality that, when the Russian Government felt it had to a certain extent recovered control of the internal situation, Count Lamsdorff, an ultra-Conservative statesman, made the extraordinary suggestion that we should work against revolutionary agitations on a common plan, pleading the necessity for monarchical solidarity. It seemed as though the loyal attitude we had maintained hitherto were not sufficient for him, and that he wanted to make use of our unimpaired strength to drag the Russian State coach out of the mud in which it had stuck, and to harness the fresh horses he demanded behind instead of in front of the vehicle. Nothing came of the suggestion, Count Lamsdorff and his reactionary colleagues having had to resign soon after making it.

The brisk and profitable trade between the two countries was another strong factor to be taken into account as tending to maintain our relations with Russia. A renewed and amplified commercial treaty would only further this, and though it was said, in individual Russian circles, that the treaty had very much favoured Germany, the answer is that, in the case of commercial treaties, such complaints are seldom lacking. In reality there was very little foundation for the complaints. They were far less the outcome of Russian opinion than of malevolent external influences to which, as became evident in other instances, the Russian mind was susceptible.

But at that time there was still reason to consider the close friendship which had existed for the last century between the reigning houses the strongest bond between Germany and Russia, as in the past. Both parties were firmly and sincerely resolved that this bond should not be relaxed. No little consideration was given to the question of strengthening it, and not a few decisions were reached with that object in view. It does not follow that the object was always attained, either because it was not made clear enough, or because one or other side did not set the right way about it.

Under these circumstances it was of great interest to see what line Russia would take at Algeciras, where the Powers were assembling for the diplomatic battle ; whether she would comply with her French ally's urgent appeal for unreserved support, or side with us. In view of Russia's having little or no interest in Morocco itself, her attitude could only be determined by considerations of high policy. At first the Russian representatives took very little active part in the Conference. Count Lamsdorff told me he considered it Russia's pleasing duty to mediate as far as possible between us and France at Algeciras, the Russian plenipotentiary had instructions to that effect. Whether the instructions were not sufficiently clear, or whether the Russian plenipotentiary did not act strictly in conformity with them, there was very little sign of effective Russian mediation at Algeciras ; on the contrary, it was evident that, as time went on, the Russian representative was more and more drawn to the French side. This would probably have been the case to a still greater degree, but for my having been able to put a spoke in the wheel through the Tsar personally. Even so, the promised Russian efforts to mediate were not made with the energy that would have been necessary in order to achieve any success.

Things were just the same with regard to the second Hague Conference, at which England was expected to propose limitation of armaments, particularly of naval construction. Some time before the meeting of the Conference was imminent, there

3

had been a change of Government in Russia in connection with the coming into force of the new Liberal Constitution. This had resulted in M. Isvolsky, a moderate Liberal, being appointed Foreign Minister in place of the reactionary Count Lamsdorff. I had been his colleague in Copenhagen, where he was the Russian Minister, and knew what he thought personally about disarmament and arbitration. Not only was his view sceptical, but also contemptuous. At the time when one of his predecessors, Count Muraviev, had electrified the world with the circular note about universal disarmament, Isvolsky was moved to remark that universal disarmament and international peace were the phantasies of Socialists and hysterical women, an expression of opinion which got him into temporary disgrace. Although he may not at heart have thought any differently, and his views may even have been strengthened by the new position in which Russia was placed as a result of the unfortunate Japanese war, and of her revolution, he could not now, as the Minister responsible for the foreign policy of the Power with whom the idea of the Conference originated, openly ridicule or object to it, all the less as it was impossible for him to shut his eyes to the fact that, beneath the fine words of the drama to be enacted at the Hague, there were thoughts far less bent on peaceable agreement between the Powers than on forming and breaking up groups, and gaining ground more likely to germinate the seeds of discord than of concord.

Under such circumstances the Minister did not turn a willing ear to our suggestion that Germany,

Austria-Hungary, and Russia, the three Imperial Powers who were brought into close touch by their equivalent interests and views, should go to the Hague hand in hand, and there jointly oppose disarmament. He seemed inclined to look on it, not only as an attempt to recast both the existing European position and the one for which the Anglo-Russian *rapprochement* was paving the way, but also as an unwelcome proposal to assume some kind of protectorship over a Russia weakened by war and revolution. It was finally necessary to resort to stronger pressure, and I was expressly instructed to make an urgent appeal to the Tsar's friendship and monarchical solidarity, in order to secure a promise to accede to our wishes.

It is well known that in consequence of our determination not to follow the English lead, which had become evident from the public discussions both in the Press and the Reichstag before the Conference, the English proposal was not debated, and a resolution was merely carried recommending the Powers to give the question of limiting armaments further consideration, just as at the first Hague Conference. This saved the Russian delegates at the Hague from having to define their attitude clearly, besides which the fact of presiding over the Conference gave them a loophole of escape. But M. Isvolsky, who was very touchy, never got over his annoyance at our having, jointly with the Austro-Hungarian ally, exerted pressure to the extent of making so unwonted an appeal to the highest quarter, an annoyance which had the effect of making him go over still more decidedly to England.

Personally, I was in so far torn in my mind as regards these events, like M. Isvolsky, that it seemed to me doubtful whether we had been wise in so clearly and explicitly declaring ourselves against disarmament. Certainly this attitude was a fresh proof of German objectivity and honesty, but would it not have been wise, from a political point of view, to have allowed the English proposal, which was only feebly supported by others, to have been discussed at the Hague, when the inevitable conclusion would have been reached that the discovery of a formula which did full justice to the geographical position and conformation, the strength of the population, the continental and overseas possessions, the internal and external, economic and political needs and necessities of all the Powers, must remain the object of pious wishes? It is true that there was the risk of the debate itself giving rise to serious and prolonged strife, but it would have been strife tempered by conventional rules, and confined within the limits of utility. For the struggle between the conflicting opinions to be carried on in the Press and the Parliaments without these conventions and limits was far more serious, and more serious still for it to be carried on secretly and surreptitiously, for the question to become more and more difficult, the position more and more strained. If the discussion had taken place at the Hague, a useful suggestion really might have been made here and there amidst the many which would have been worthless, and even if, as was to be expected, a solution of the great problem had not been found, still a great step forward would have been taken, if only in the manifestation of goodwill. We should have secured an attentive hearing and valuable partisans when representing our own and the general possibilities and impossibilities, and adducing reasons in support of our arguments, and should not have incurred the cruel odium, which was exploited by our opponents to our undoing, of having quenched the feeble spark of life in the pacifist bantling.

I cannot recall without the deepest regret the fact that I was not destined to be more than an observant witness of the gradual *rapprochement* between Russia and England.   English politicians had been shrewd enough to recognise long since that a Russia plunging into adventures and coming to grief in them, must not only suffer considerable loss of strength as England's ancient foe, but might also be drawn into the magic circle of British interests without much difficulty, if suitable advances were made.   The upshot of the war and of the revolution proved the correctness of this calculation.   Beginning cautiously, but acting more and more openly, as the success of her policy became more evident, England deliberately set herself to give her tottering adversary proofs of goodwill, and to hold out the attractive prospect of replacing the old enmity by a new and valuable friendship.   The constitutional turmoil which followed the Russian revolution was turned to account with consummate skill, and by well-tried methods of procedure, in order to get England extolled in her own and the easily accessible Russian Press, as the stronghold of ideal Liberal political life.   Soon after the constitutional change in Russia, the feeling for England had become so much warmer that there was a question of a further step, a cautious knock at the Government door—in diplomatic language this is called "sounding." But before this step could be taken, it was forestalled by a proposal from the Russian side that there should be an understanding as to disputed points. This allowed of negotiations being started at once, with a view to formulating mutual guarantees against further feuds between the two Powers in Persia, Afghanistan and Thibet.

M. Isvolsky had made a point of telling me quite frankly, from the beginning, what his reasons had been for embarking on a new foreign policy, and for asking his Imperial master to authorise his carrying on corresponding negotiations. The Tsar had been very reluctant to agree to this, but had given the authority. Russia was so enfeebled after her defeat in the East, and after the revolution, which was by no means at an end, that a continuance of England's former hostility, represented a danger to Russia of such magnitude that it was essential to set about doing away with it in good earnest, and without delay. Hard as it might be from the standpoint of self-reliance, there was no choice but to make an effort to bridge over the differences by means of a friendly understanding. The chances had been in favour of the negotiations leading to a satisfactory conclusion from the beginning, but in view of the difficulties which had no less to be considered, it would be premature to speak with any confidence He wished to lay, stress on the fact that there was no idea of a general *rapprochement* and of leaning on England, of shifting the Russian helm and steering in the English course ; the understanding was, on the contrary, only to relate to definite points, which had hitherto been points of dispute. An agreement as to the delimitation of spheres of influence in Persia was contemplated, without prejudice to the political independence and economic freedom of the country ; also an agreement as to the maintenance of the *status quo* in Afghanistan. England would probably demand due recognition of her exceptional position in the Persian Gulf, but in this respect he meant to defend Russia's interests very firmly. He could all the less agree to her being deprived of all prospect of access to the open sea in that direction, as she had now been cut off from it in the Asiatic East. None of the parties concerned contemplated prejudicing German interests and rights in any way, this he must repeat, in view of the anxiety that seemed to be felt by the general public in Germany, and the rash statements made by the English and Russian Press. The proposed Anglo-Russian agreement did not in the least represent a new move directed against Germany. As to this the contracting parties had been of one mind from the first, and the maintenance of this principle was one of the prior conditions of the negotiations.

There is no doubt that M. Isvolsky was sincere when he insisted that the *rapprochement* to England must not be accepted as a renunciation of the tried German friendship, still less as a hostile move. There have been proofs of his sincerity. Both he and the Tsar were of opinion that the understanding which was limited to definitely circumscribed points, was absolutely compatible with the friendly relationship to Germany. The agreement was accordingly concluded in August 1907, its scope being limited and the purport as described. There was nothing in the wording of the draft which could be interpreted as opening the door to an understanding in further geographical and general political spheres. M. Isvolsky again took the opportunity of protesting that we had no cause for anxiety. On the contrary, he declared that he was prepared to conclude an agreement with us too; it would concern railway construction in Persia in connection with the Bagdad railway. I was able to reach an understanding with him as to the main features of this agreement, but was prevented from carrying it any further by my appointment to be Minister for Foreign Affairs The treaty was only concluded a few years later with Isvolsky's successor, Sazonov, and signed on the occasion of the Tsar's visit to Potsdam in the autumn of 1910. We had first to overcome Russian prejudices with regard to our supposed designs in Persia, and to weather the Bosnian crisis with its after effects On this occasion the new Russian Minister was also profuse in his assurances of the most friendly intentions, and entered into an understanding to the effect that neither of the two Powers " would embark on anything which might be aimed against the other." As far as I know, however, this agreement was never put into writing and signed. I also reached what was at first merely a roughly outlined understanding as to an agreement to maintain the *status quo* in the Baltic, shortly before I left St. Petersburg. In this instance the suggestion also came from M. Isvolsky, who obviously tried to keep up the connection with us.

It is true that outside the circle of those responsible for the Anglo-Russian agreement, it was interpreted and welcomed as an event of political importance extending far beyond its limited purport, directly it was concluded. People talked of a very promising first step in the direction of a fresh grouping of Powers directed against Germany, and here and there even spoke of a Triple Alliance. It was M. Isvolsky's habit at that time to shrug his shoulders when these things were alluded to, and say that such talk was unwarrantable, an *entente* between Russia, France and England was merely a vision conjured up by an imaginative Press; in reality it did not exist, nor was it contemplated. This may have been true at that time, but it did not remain so. In reality, as time went on, there were signs that not only the Press but also the statesmen of the Western Powers wished to draw Russia gradually into their orbit, and the wish ultimately resolved itself into deeds.

M. Isvolsky had at first opposed some resistance to such overtures, in accordance with the Tsar's instructions. He hesitated and postponed, but in course of time he became more complaisant. This complaisance increased in proportion as the Minister responsible for Russia's foreign policy was forced to recognise that the Russian Empire's progress on the new road to expansion on which it proposed to embark after the Asiatic East had been barred and bolted, the road to Constantinople, threatened to be impeded if not barred by the ever increasing firmness of our friendship for Turkey, and Austria-Hungary's more energetic procedure in the Balkans under Count Aehrenthal's guidance. If the road to Constantinople, "via Berlin and Vienna," seemed to him no longer practicable, it must necessarily, become worth his while to endeavour to reach the goal by another road and with other help He could not have failed to realise that this policy was not to be achieved without great difficulties, that Austria-Hungary would not readily be dislodged from the Balkans, and could rely, on Germany's powerful help in this matter.

The differences existed, they threatened to become more and more serious, a conflict in due course appeared inevitable. Russia began by feeling that she was too disabled to fight, but this conclusion was just what finally led to her making an effort to gain time in which to recover her strength, and to her accepting proffered help from outside. There can hardly be any doubt that this was the true explanation of the meeting between the Tsar and the King of England and their Ministers at Reval in June 1908, which was intended to confirm and strengthen the Anglo-Russian understanding reached about a year earlier, although here again we were expressly assured that nothing had been discussed, let alone promised, which could be detrimental to Germany.

It has occasionally, been publicly, remarked in Germany, in terms of reproach, that it was a pity, nothing adequate was done on our side in St. Petersburg to oppose the *rapprochement* to England in good time. The answer to this is that the best means of doing so would have been to do away with all that compelled Russian policy to turn to England. This was all the less in our power, as the Anglo-Russian agreement dealt with questions quite outside our sphere of interests and influence. Under the circumstances, even if the reassuring Russian protestations did not satisfy us, our influence could only consist in accentuating and carefully cultivating the friendly relations which were based on the traditional dynastic tie. Nothing was omitted in this direction. Moreover, an important and drastic move on the chessboard of high policy would have been the only means of arresting the new course. The time for that had gone by. Experience of the Björko agreement had shown what to expect from setting to work with nothing but diplomatic language and ideas, and counting on goodwill.

Domestic policy was more the centre of gravity of political life in Russia, immediately after the revolutionary chaos, and during the state of ferment caused by the formation, procedure, and dissolution of the Imperial Duma, than in normal times. The official German representative had to adopt a strictly neutral attitude towards it on general principles. The Russian Government, especially M. Isvolsky, was particularly sensitive on this point, and inclined to draw the line dividing foreign from domestic policy, which was not always clearly discernible, and very often bewildering, in favour of the latter. Thus, for instance, the Minister would not at first listen to a representation I was instructed to make to him, namely, that the extraordinary severity of the Russian Government towards the

Jewish portion of the population drove large numbers of Jews as refugees over the frontier, so that our towns and villages were seriously overcrowded. He looked on it as an unwarrantable interference in domestic matters, and it was difficult to convince him that matters of this kind, which affect both parties, require combined consideration   I told him that, in our experience, the Russian Governments had, as a rule, taken a very broad view when it was a question of checking the immigration of what appeared to them undesirable German elements into Russia.

The Liberal Party in Russia did its best, not without considerable backing up from outside, to represent that the German Embassy was very ready to exert its strong influence in a reactionary sense ; in particular it acted as intermediary, and promoted a brisk correspondence between the Kaiser and the Tsar.   That was a wilful invention, with a distinct purpose.   No letter or telegram from the Kaiser to the Tsar passed through my hands, nor did I ever receive instructions to discuss Russian domestic matters with the highest quarter, or venture to do anything of the kind on my own account.   It is a well-known fact that the Kaiser and the Tsar corresponded personally, a fact which ought not to be thought surprising.   It is equally a matter of course that political matters were alluded to in this correspondence.   But even the keenest critic could hardly see anything in the nature of mis- placed attempts to exert influence, particularly in a reactionary sense, in the Kaiser's letters to the Tsar which have been published since.

The hope cherished by those in power that the

Russian Empire's domestic position would materially improve when the Liberal Constitution came into force was not fulfilled. The elections to the first Imperial Duma passed off comparatively quietly, it is true, and the Tsar, who came to the capital from the peace of Tsarkoë Selo for the first time for two years, was able to open the Duma in solemn state in the Winter Palace, but the Parliament itself soon proved to be less a solid support of the new superstructure than the rallying point of disintegrating passions and subversive forces. In a very short time the Duma embarked on a revolutionary course, and had to be dissolved. From this time onwards constant efforts were again made to bring about a revolution, and isolated, horrible crimes were perpetrated. The capital was continually under "special protection," outwardly recognisable by the number of police and troops called out, and occasional Cossack outbreaks.

This state of affairs made it very difficult for me to fulfil one of my duties of a ceremonial nature—holding the usual first reception. Not only in monarchical, but in almost all States which receive and send Ambassadors, it has been customary from time immemorial, and still is very usual, for a newly arrived Ambassador to give those whose acquaintance he proposes making in his official capacity an opportunity of paying him the first formal visit, as the representative of his Sovereign, or of the sovereignty of his countrymen. Logically, the new Ambassador should make an arrangement of the kind immediately after his arrival, but, as a rule, there are extraneous obstacles in the way of it, and therefore the claim in this respect has been generally, ignored.   Nowhere was the custom of formal ambassadorial receptions—the Italian word *ricivimiento* was used in speaking of them—and an etiquette which prescribed certain forms and ceremonies for such functions, more firmly adhered to than at the Russian Court.   True, the invitations were sent in the Ambassador's name, but they, were issued from the office of the Russian Master of the Ceremonies, and confined exclusively to members of the Court and official world   Personal acquaintances outside these circles could not be invited   Besides this the ceremony, at which those taking part in it had to appear in full uniform or Court dress, could not take place until the Ambassador and his wife had been more or less formally received, not only by their Russian Majesties, but also by all the Grand Dukes and Grand Duchesses   These formalities in themselves took up no little time, and when they, were got through the reception had to be postponed again and again, on account of the unsatisfactory, conditions of public safety in the capital.   It was only, possible to think of fulfilling this obligation about a year after I entered on my, duties as Ambassador, and even then it still seemed rather a risk.   Thanks to extensive precautionary measures, the ceremony finally took place without any *contretemps*.

It gives me special pleasure to be able to speak with gratitude and satisfaction of the high and influential position held by, the Germans in St. Petersburg, Moscow, and other towns, and the friendly and active relations between them and the official representative of their country.   Their settlements were numerous, stronger than those of any other foreign nation, they were held in great esteem, and were remarkable for their *esprit de corps*, which had frequently been put to the test. Most of the members of these settlements were prosperous, an'd held leading positions in commerce and industry. They were far ahead of all other nationalities, and a brilliant example to them in cultural undertakings, works of charity, and patriotism. The official German representative could but feel proud and happy to be at the head of such Germanism.

There were many thousand other Germans domiciled in Russia, for whom, according to the principles of international law, the official representative could do nothing, for they were Russian subjects. These were the so-called colonists, who, summoned by Catherine the Great in days gone by, had settled in the Russian Empire, chiefly on the Volga and Dnieper, where they had founded flourishing communities and retained the German language and German customs. The same applied to the Baltic Germans, who had been longer and more firmly incorporated in the Russian State. Both these, who were only Germans at heart, and those who were subjects of the German Empire, were, generally speaking, on good terms with the Russians by whom they were surrounded. The happy relations were merely temporarily prejudiced at the time of the revolutionary outbreak. Only a small group—the German-Catholic community in St. Petersburg—had to complain of any annoyance, and this was from the Poles. As it was less a question of denominational than of national interest, I had warmly espoused the cause

of the little community, and, thanks to the friendly
spirit shown by the Russian Government, had been
able to help them to obtain recognition of their independence, and the concession of a chapel of their
own, just as, when I was Councillor of Embassy in
Paris, I had given my attention to the establishment
of the German Evangelical community on a firm
basis, and the building of a German Church,
equally for national reasons.

On the frequent occasions when I had to enter
into political matters with the Tsar personally, I
had invariably found him thoroughly conversant
with the concomitant questions, and willing to
discuss them frankly and thoroughly, even when he
could not have been specially prepared, a proof
that those who, rejecting the generally accepted
view, gave the Sovereign credit for a very considerable amount of political knowledge and ability,
and above all for being extremely conscientious
and industrious and possessing a strong sense
of duty, were perfectly right. He had also the
gift of grasping salient points rapidly and
correctly, and a certain quickness of repartee. A
courteous manner, and calm almost dispassionate
attitude, even towards exciting questions, made a
pleasant impression, and facilitated the conferences.
His misfortune was the lack of self-confidence, a
quality closely associated with a certain diffidence
and humility, which made him slow and irresolute
in his decisions, and susceptible to the most conflicting influences. As a rule, the influence of those
to whom it had fallen to have the last opportunity
of talking to him personally, carried the day.

In reality his was a simple character, not liable

to be swayed by powerful impulses or way-
ward passions of any kind, although by no
means strong or self-reliant. Anything rather
than a typical Emperor, on the other hand, an
exemplary husband and father, only happy in the
bosom of his family, and happiest in the nursery.
The strong tendency to mysticism and fatalism,
which at times asserted itself disastrously, was a
true Russian inheritance. It was a curious fact
that the mystical tendencies were more strongly
developed in the Tsarina than in the Tsar.

The cruel pitilessness with which the Tsar was
credited was not consistent with what was in reality
a kind heart ; it was not natural to him, on the contrary, it was due to pernicious influences, to the in-
fatuated idea, traditional among the ruling caste
in Russia, that the ruler's power was only absolute
in the eyes of the moujik when it extended to disposing of the subject's life and death without a
sign of feeling, with the inflexible calm of a graven
image. The Tsar's inability to resist baneful influences of this kind was primarily responsible for
the disaster which has befallen the Russian
Empire, and the cruelly tragic fate which awaited
him and his.

My duties brought me into constant touch both
with the Foreign Minister, Count Lamsdorff, his
successor, M. Isvolsky, and the Prime Ministers,
Count Witte and M. Stolypin. Count Lamsdorff
was a man whose thoughts and actions were
rooted in the old Russian régime. He was wont
to adopt an attitude of somewhat benevolent con-
descension towards the other Powers, while at heart
his only political principle was that of autocratic

4

despotism. His Conservatism, and the traditional friendship between the Courts, attracted him to us, but he thought himself of so much importance that he hardly looked on us as more than an obliging friend whose services might be accepted without any obligation to do an equivalent service in return. He did not like France, both on account of her being Red, and a creditor. But the alliance with the Republic was a card in the game of Russian policy he would not part with. England was to him the ancient foe. Austria-Hungary was nearest his heart, as a centre of Conservative political life under aristocratic leadership. M. Isvolsky's views did not originally differ materially from those of his predecessor, but he was far more versatile, ambitious, pliable, and apt to change. The sense in which his point of view first underwent a change, in the face of a new situation, was that he held out the olive branch to England, the ancient foe, and turned away from Austria-Hungary, who stood in the way of his plans with regard to Constantinople, therewith turning away from us at the same time. The alienation resolved itself into hostility later on, after his diplomatic defeat in the Bosnian crisis.

Count Witte was one of the few Russian statesmen who realised betimes the necessity for counteracting the internal revolutionary movement by striking out Liberal paths. He even made the attempt, but met with no little opposition, particularly at Court. It is true that he was the author of the " October Manifesto," in which the Tsar gave Russia a Magna Charta, but he was not privileged to guide the first steps taken by the Russian State in the new era. The Tsar, who did not like him

on account of his lack of polish and a certain
tendency to act as mentor, and would not entrust
him with a greater degree of power, parted with
him at the moment when the first Imperial Duma
met. During the short life of the Duma, the reins
of Government were in the hands of M. Goremykin,
a Conservative, who, it is true, included a few
Liberal Ministers among his colleagues, but personally was obviously appointed in order to act as
a drag on any tendency the Duma might show
to lapse into Radicalism, a rôle in which he was
unsuccessful.

His successor was M. Stolypin, who restored the
shattered State authority by grasping it firmly
without becoming reactionary, and tried to allay
the excitement and turn men's thoughts in another
direction by bringing in a measure of land reform
on a great scale for the benefit of the peasants.
It is well known that he was the object of a sinister
bomb attack, made on his private house, when
several of his family were seriously injured, and
many people killed. He himself escaped unhurt in
a marvellous way, an incident which made a strong
impression in his favour on the superstitious
moujiks.

The Minister of Finance, Kokovzev, must also be
mentioned among eminent statesmen of that period.
I owed the prompt and courteous adjustment of
rather a difficult case to my friendly personal
relations with this very Germanophil Minister.
Shortly before the Russo-German commercial treaty
came into force, with its increased customs duties,
goods had been sent in large quantities from
Germany to Russia in order to avoid these duties.

Many of the goods did not cross the frontier in time, owing to the inadequacy of the Russian railway system, a circumstance which led to the German commercial circles concerned making complaints, which were urged in the Press and in the Reichstag. I was instructed to try to secure them against loss. The question of title was at best doubtful ; to pursue the matter from the legal point of view held out more prospect of endless negotiations than of a satisfactory result. I therefore dealt with it by appealing to reason, and obtained from M. Kokovzev the prompt concession of compensation which far exceeded all expectations. At that time the tendency to depreciate the diplomatic representatives, which became more marked later on, was already apparent. They were said to be lacking in knowledge of political economy, and in ability to achieve tangible results. Loud as the complaints had been of the difficulties which had arisen on the Russian frontier, very little public notice was now taken in Germany of their satisfactory adjustment. Psychologically, this is easily accounted for, but the fact is regrettable in so far as it meant that a refutation of the theory that diplomacy is useless was thrown away.

Of the representatives of other Powers who were my colleagues in St. Petersburg, the Austro-Hungarian Ambassador, Baron (afterwards Count) Aehrenthal, and his successor, Count Berchtold, seem worthy of special notice. Baron Aehrenthal, whose views were ultra-Conservative, found great difficulty in getting on with the new Minister, Isvolsky, and was too well acquainted with the aims and practices of Russian policy, from long observation at close quarters, not to be its opponent. He could not bring himself to make a fresh effort to bridge over the differences, as had been done years before in the Murzteg agreement; he no longer looked on the Russian colossus with the feet of clay as the Power whose pressure it would be advisable to avoid; the time appeared to him to have come for Austria-Hungary to refuse to be pushed out of her natural sphere of influence in the Balkans, and to act boldly, even at the risk of serious conflict, relying both on her own hitherto dormant, but still vital, strength, and on the help of the German ally.

The calculation proved correct, but Baron Aehrenthal's political foresight did not go far enough to see that if Russia were to meet with powerful resistance and be forced to retreat, she would be all the more keenly bent on getting help from other quarters, and would resume the interrupted march to the goal she had persistently pursued—Constantinople—with greater energy, as soon as she felt she had recovered sufficient strength. As Baron Aehrenthal's successor in St. Petersburg, Count Berchtold witnessed the development of the Anglo-Russian *rapprochement* without adopting any attitude towards it other than that of a spectator. In Vienna he carried on the Aehrenthal policy of fighting over the Balkans. It is well known that the fire ignited in the Balkans led to the devastating conflagration of the World War.

Sir Arthur Nicholson, who had made himself conspicuous at Algeciras as one of our most dogged opponents, was Great Britain's vigilant representative in St. Petersburg, where it fell to his lot to conduct the negotiations over the understanding in Asiatic questions. In the course of these negotiations he too repeatedly, told me that no thought unfriendly to Germany was associated with them, and he took pains to add the assurance that he personally, had no antagonistic feeling whatever to Germany, an insistence which reminded me of a well-known French proverb.

The French Ambassador, M. Maurice Bompard, a man with an extensive knowledge of business, particularly in the economic sphere, and a simple, almost shy manner, in this way, differing very much from his versatile and socially brilliant predecessor, Count Montebello, did not find it easy to adopt an attitude consistent with the relations which to a certain extent arose naturally from the fact of the alliance. He gave dissatisfaction, which led to disagreement with M. Isvolsky, and soon after that to his recall, by the way, in which he furthered French industrial penetration, particularly by making expeditions to the Donetz coalfields without the consent of the Russian Government, and also by inopportune attempts to influence the Liberal " Cadet " Party in the Duma. The incident is instructive as regards the limits to which diplomatic activity, is restricted.

I did not remain very, long in St. Petersburg. After little more than a year and a half I was appointed Minister for Foreign Affairs.

III

SECRETARY OF STATE FOR FOREIGN AFFAIRS

IN the autumn of 1907, I was appointed Secretary of State for Foreign Affairs in succession to Herr von Tschirschky, whose health was no longer equal to the work. To me the appointment was as unwelcome as it was unexpected. After having held what were in many ways specially pleasant foreign posts for a number of years, and risen to be an Ambassador—according to international law the personal representative of the Sovereign,—a position which combines much that is peculiarly delightful with its unusual distinction, it was not easy to take over an office with no special privileges, and whose drawbacks outweighed its advantages. The burden of this office was so great that it had already been too much for more than one Minister. Freiherr von Richthofen, the type of man who enjoyed work, had broken down hopelessly, and Herr von Tschirschky had found it necessary to resign, in order to save his health from giving way entirely.

I was less afraid of the extent than of the importance of the business. I was hardly a novice in foreign affairs, but there was a good deal in the new position of which I knew nothing. It was no longer a question, as in foreign posts, of acting in accordance with instructions and suggestions, and of one's activity being confined to the locality. Instead of carrying out I now had to lead, to rule over a department which was comprehensive enough within, and which extended over th'e world without. In addition to this there was the defective organisation of the Foreign Office, an inheritance from former days, of which I was to a certain extent aware. True, the Secretary of State had the Under-Secretary, directors of departments, and trustworthy Councillors to assist him, but there was no help of that kind in the political department, just the one of most importance. It was under the sole direction of the Secretary of State, but would have needed a man at the head of it who would give his time exclusively to the political business, who had been long enough in the office to be familiar with the work, and the method of dealing with it, and had not to direct the whole, like the Secretary of State, who was so overburdened with his multifarious duties, attendance at Court, at the Federal Council and Reichstag, at Ministries and the Prussian Diet, intercourse with foreign diplomats, and unavoidable social obligations, that he had not the time necessary for undisturbed solid work, for going deeply into important matters. There was no need for the political assistant to be so unusual a personality as Herr von Holstein, who for that matter was never formally a " political Director." He was only a " reporting Councillor," but he had managed to acquire quite a peculiar influence, which was sometimes very annoying, not only to the Secretaries of

State, but also to the Chancellors, and by no means always salutary.

The thought of my parliamentary duties also rather alarmed me .It is not given to everyone to be able to appear before a solemn assembly of critical hearers and make speeches, often without preparation, which the busy telegraph wires send out to the world at once, to be always ready to answer questions which, more in the Reichstag than in any other Parliament, relate to the most private political transactions, the minutest details of administration, and the most trivial acts and omissions of the foreign representatives. The course usually pursued by English Ministers, of either giving short evasive replies to inconvenient questions, or not answering them at all, was not practicable in the Reichstag. Prince Bulow's kind promise to help me with his superior knowledge, qualifications, and experience, gave me some encouragement to accept the onerous office, and when all was said and done I had no choice, for the feeling that perhaps some-one else would have been more equal to the task would hardly have been considered a reason for refusing.

Before taking over the official business, I took the opportunity of making sure that my view of the duties and of the. policy to be pursued was the same as the Chancellor's. I started on the assumption that the Chancellor's representative in the sphere of foreign affairs ought not to carry on any policy other than that prescribed by the responsible head. This was the only attitude that seemed to me consistent with the idea of representation. The relation between Imperial Chancellor and Secretary of State was not really that of a superior towards a subordinate, it was closer, to a certain extent that of personal alliance. If my personal opinion differed from the Chancellor's I was not only entitled to uphold it, but it was even more my duty to do so. I should have no right, however, to go so far as to insist on it. In case of differences of opinion, and of its being impossible to reconcile them, the only way out of the difficulty would be either to sacrifice my convictions or resign.

Such differences, however, did not arise. The first exhaustive conference showed that we entirely agreed in thinking it important to maintain and strengthen Germany's position in the midst of a world for the most part ill-disposed towards her, not by rattling the sabre and using threatening language, but by quietly pursuing our own way. The differences between us and France and England were the principal elements of unrest in Europe ; in the one case Alsace-Lorraine, in the other, position in the world and naval construction. These differences could only be settled by an unworthy capitulation on our part, by our sacrificing vital interests. This was not to be thought of for a moment. All we could do would be to make an effort to tone down the sharpness of the differences, to diminish the sources of friction, bring about understandings on other than the burning questions, and generally allay the distrust of us which existed on all sides. Prince Bülow particularly agreed as to the desirability of winning the confidence of the smaller neighbouring States, and achieving general harmony in this indirect way. Moreover, we were of one mind as to the advisability of keeping in closer touch with the Reichstag in questions of foreign policy than had been the custom hitherto. It was further decided to act with the strictest impartiality, and in accordance with the spirit of the times, in selecting foreign representatives and making other appointments.

I took over the management of the Foreign Office on November 4, 1907. At first I still had the help of the Under-Secretary, von Muhlberg, a most able man, who had been selected for the post of Prussian Minister at the Vatican. Later on, Stemrich, the Minister in Teheran, took his place.

Hardly had I been initiated into the official business when I had to accompany the Emperor to England, on a visit, with the Empress, to the English Court. Apart from the visit being a duty, as a matter of courtesy, it was hoped that it might rouse a feeling likely to conduce to an improvement in our relations to England. These relations were no longer what they had been in the days of Queen Victoria, and of the Prime Ministers, Lord Beaconsfield and Lord Salisbury. They were correct as between one Government and another, but lacked warmth. The first coolness had arisen during the Boer War. The British Government recognised with some gratitude that we had not selfishly added to the difficulty of England's position, but public opinion had taken the German people's enthusiasm for the Boer cause very much amiss. The well-known Kruger telegram had had the effect of a cold-water douche. Now that we had become England's successful rival in world trade, and particularly now that we had begun to build a strong fleet, the British Empire felt uneasy, felt her vital interests menaced, and adopted a more and more unfriendly attitude towards us. England entered into an *entente cordiale* with France, and was about to draw Russia into her orbit. An extremely active press considered it a duty to poison the atmosphere of the relations to Germany more and more. True, there was opposition to this in England itself ; well-meaning circles tried to keep up pleasant ties with Germany in cultural spheres, but attempts of this kind to reach a better understanding had no substantial influence on the fundamental feeling of the two nations, and did not succeed in bridging over the differences.

The visit was a success which exceeded all expectations. The Kaiser's speech at the first State dinner at Windsor Castle, when he spoke with great feeling of the recollections of his youth, and of his veneration for the departed " great Queen," was the prelude to extremely cordial intercourse between the illustrious English and German personages. King Edward and Queen Alexandra repeatedly spoke most warmly of the pleasure the visit, and the friendly feeling shown by the Kaiser, gave them. His reception by the populace was also marked by a cordiality far beyond ordinary courtesy. The public had gathered with great satisfaction from the Kaiser's first speech, that strong ties attached him to English life, and felt that he sincerely and earnestly wished for the restoration of a better understanding between the two nations. London acclaimed their Imperial Majesties when they drove through the city, on an extraordinarily beautiful autumn day, to be the guests of the citizens in the Mansion House, in accordance with ancient custom. Fuel was added to the flame of enthusiasm by what the Kaiser said in reply to the Lord Mayor's address of welcome, namely, that what had given him special pleasure, and deeply touched him on the drive through the gaily decorated streets, had been seeing the reproduction in large letters of the saying : " Blood is thicker than water." Then again the Kaiser's speech at the banquet, on the friendly feeling for England which predominated in Germany, and the general wish for cordial relations, made an overwhelming impression. Sir Edward Grey, the British Foreign Minister, who sat next to me, was obviously touched, and we promised one another, shaking hands warmly, to do all in our power to act in the sense of the Kaiser's speech.

It was customary at the English Court to invite Ministers and other prominent personages to Windsor Castle in groups, and thus give them an opportunity of having informal conversations with the Kaiser. Although on this occasion our idea had been that the visit should, in itself, have a good effect, and accordingly definite agreements had not been contemplated, still it was quite natural that political questions should be referred to in the conversations with English statesmen. As a rule, such discussions did not take place unless either I or the Ambassador, Count Metternich, were present. If this happened not to be practicable, owing to extraneous circumstances, the Kaiser did not fail to tell us exactly what had passed as soon as possible. Very often he had no opportunity of doing so till late at night, after the State entertainments.

The chief question at issue between us and

England, that of naval construction, was of too
delicate a nature to be more than lightly touched
upon.   On the other hand, the Bagdad railway
was a subject which could be frankly discussed,
with a view to bringing about an agreement.   It
was well known that England did not favour this
project, as she thought the overland route to
India would imperil important interests.   Individual
English statesmen, for instance the Secretary of
State for India, went so far as to fear that if
Germany had sole control of the railway she might
be in a position to push forward troops towards
India.   This question could only be settled by
giving England a share in the control.   The Kaiser
therefore proposed our constructing the terminal
section of the line, up to the Persian Gulf, jointly ;
the terminus, the harbour, might be under English
control, on condition that the " door should always
remain open for peaceable purposes."   The proposal roused great interest, and was well received
on the English side.   Lord Haldane, the English
War Minister, who strongly favoured friendly
Anglo-German relations, submitted it to his friend
Sir Edward Grey at once, strongly recommending its acceptance.   Sir Edward was also quite
open to the idea, and gave me an opportunity of
talking the matter over with him.   He proposed
that we should discuss the details jointly, but
added a wish that the French and Russians should
take part in the discussion, with a view to the
problem being satisfactorily solved from every point
of view.   We did not think we could agree to this
without imperilling our position.   We should have
found ourselves alone at the conference table

against three Powers acting together, and not favourably disposed to us. Neither did it seem advisable to give Russia and France reason to take for granted that we were inclined to attach the same importance to their interest in the matter, which was very small, as to that of England, who was far more deeply concerned. It was also doubtful whether Sir Edward Grey's wish that these two Powers should take part in the Conference was only prompted by the idea of a general settlement, or whether he might not also be influenced by a desire that a new grouping of Powers, at that time only dimly discernible, the Triple Alliance which afterwards came clearly to light, should be more or less openly recognised. Consequently nothing further was done in the matter, and it gradually lapsed.

After the ten days' visit to Windsor the Kaiser went to Highcliffe Castle, which had been rented for him, to recover from an obstinate catarrh in the mild English south coast climate. I returned to my official business in Berlin.

The next important task that devolved on me was the conclusion of an agreement guaranteeing the territorial *status quo* in the North Sea, in conjunction with a similar treaty with regard to the Baltic. The idea of the latter had originated with M. Isvolsky, with whom it seemed to be mainly a question of pacifying Sweden, who had been alarmed by the Russian undertakings in the Aaland Islands and on the Scandinavian ocean coast. The North Sea agreement had been projected in the Foreign Office before my time, and was the outcome of a wish to give England in the first instance, and then the world in general, a proof of our pacific intentions, and thereby to promote European peace. Both schemes were suggested by the agreements England had concluded with Spain and France with regard to the Atlantic and Mediterranean coasts. The British Government showed no hesitation in agreeing to our proposal of negotiations over the North Sea agreement, but adopted the same attitude as in the matter of the Bagdad railway, and proposed that the agreement should include all the States which had North Sea coasts, instead of being restricted to Germany and England, as we had intended. This gave the matter quite a different aspect, it diminished the value of the agreement as far as we were concerned, " the wine was watered." All the same we were able to fall in with the English suggestion, remembering that, although it was not what we had originally intended, still, an agreement on a broader basis might contribute to dispel the distrust of us felt by our greater and smaller neighbours, and in this way be beneficial to our relations with England.

It is doubtful whether Sir Edward Grey's wish that the treaty should be extended originated in a sincere desire for general pacification, or in a possible disinclination to enter into agreements with us alone, which might give the impression of a political *rapprochement*. Be that as it may, we could not drop the threads of the project which had been set on foot without arousing suspicion, and the fact that the Baltic agreement ran parallel with it was a further argument in favour of acceding to the English wish. Consequently, we entered into negotiations with the North Sea States, Sweden, Denmark, and the Netherlands, as well as with England. There was no need to consider Norway, as she had concluded treaties of neutrality not long before, or Belgium, whose existence and neutrality were guaranteed by the Powers.

It was doubtful whether France could be considered one of the North Sea States. She had only a short line of coast, and one harbour, Dunkirk. But she herself expressed a wish to take part in the proceedings, on the ground that she had been one of the signatories to the North Sea Fisheries agreement. Although this was rather far-fetched, there was no reasonable excuse for refusing, and we were thus involved in negotiations with five States, which were protracted, because of the requests for explanations, and proposals of slight alterations made first by one and then by another. Some difficulty was also caused by its being desired that the North Sea and Baltic agreements should be as nearly as possible on the same lines, and signed at the same time. At the eleventh hour, when everything was in readiness for the North Sea agreement to be signed in Berlin, the Dutch and Danish delegates suggested rather shyly that a few words recognising neutrality should be inserted in the text of the agreement. I remarked that, in view of the obviously pacific character of the agreement, such an addition seemed unnecessary. It was open to both States, in virtue of their sovereignty, to declare themselves neutral at any time, either once for all, or judging each case on its own merits. If the suggestion was that all the North Sea States should recognise permanent neutrality, and in this way introduce an element of International law into the agreement, that would be a matter which could not be settled off-hand, as though it were a mere trifle.   It would require fresh consideration and negotiations between the States interested, both in the Baltic and North Sea agreements.   I was willing to abandon the agreement now awaiting signature, and start fresh negotiations, but if this were to be done I must ask that the suggestion be formulated in writing with reasons in support of it.   On this the delegates immediately withdrew the motion, and told me in confidence that the idea had not originated with them or their leading Ministers ; it had emanated from the somewhat excited imagination of the Dutch Minister in Copenhagen.   This Minister was recalled by his Government shortly afterwards, and, as he continued to urge the neutrality question in public, was retired into private life.

The Baltic agreement was signed in St. Petersburg on April 23, 1908, and the North Sea agreement in Berlin simultaneously.   The agreements gave satisfaction on all sides, particularly to the smaller States, where they were justly regarded as a solemn declaration of pacific intentions, and welcomed accordingly.   Sweden was extremely thankful to be relieved of her anxiety, with regard to the Aaland Islands.   France, also, appeared very satisfied with the settlement, which, as the French Ambassador pointed out, was the first politically important agreement concluded with Germany since the Franco-Prussian War.   Whether a certain satisfaction that the North Sea agreement we proposed had not been concluded with England alone did not play some part in this, is a question which may be asked, but cannot be answered, for lack of convincing proof.

The objections made by the responsible heads of our Navy, who thought the agreements would' prejudice their freedom of action, in case of war, also very nearly prevented their being concluded We succeeded, however, in silencing these objections. Later on it became generally known that our Navy was rather inclined to hold political opinions of its own, and to pursue a policy, which did not always coincide with that pursued by the Ministry for Foreign Affairs; in fact, was sometimes directly opposed to it. True, there could only be one opinion as to the great fundamental principle that the Navy, just the same as the Army, should be a means to great ends, not an object in itself, and that hence military policy must to a certain extent depend on the general policy. Nor could there be any disagreement as to the rate of naval construction, this having been practically fixed for many years to come by the Navy Bill. On the other hand, there is no doubt that the way in which everything relating to the Navy and its growing strength was publicly, discussed in Germany, the noisy interest shown by wide circles of the people in the development of our naval power, an interest aroused and encouraged by active propaganda, and the spirit which prevailed in the Navy and sometimes led to unfortunate utterances, furnished other countries with food for suspicion, intensified the differences between us and England, and' made it very difficult for those responsible for our foreign policy, to achieve their aims.

If this led to disagreement between the Foreign Office and the Navy it cannot be a matter of surprise, for it was only natural. The Navy is, like the Army, a fighting force, an embodiment of national strength, seeking satisfaction, not in rest, but in activity. It is animated by a spirit essentially different to that of the Foreign Office, a spirit of undaunted determination, of conscious strength delighting in great deeds, rather than of slow and deliberate reflection and action. But the essential difference of disposition was not an end of the matter; the eagerness to accomplish something great led to the Navy pursuing a policy of its own, even at the risk of inconvenience to the foreign political circles. This, however, was not a state of affairs peculiar to Germany. The relations between the Navy and the Foreign Office are apt to be more or less distant, if not strained, in other countries too. The fact that individual units of the Navy are not infrequently entrusted with political tasks, even in peace time, and that, thanks to the strong impression they are able to make, they solve difficulties more promptly and thoroughly than can be done by the efforts of diplomacy, and the further fact that naval officers have an opportunity of becoming acquainted with other countries in important matters, and of gaining an insight into the life there, and particularly into the life of the colonists, by whom they are hospitably entertained and fêted, easily leads them to feel confidence in their own judgment in political matters, and produces a tendency to act on their own responsibility.

It must be admitted that instances of this have

been more pronounced in Germany, than in other countries. Our Navy was a comparatively new achievement, born of the spirit of youth and growing strength, planned and carried out by a master hand. It was, in an even greater degree than the Army, the pride of the nation, an organisation which powerfully appealed to national sentiment. The military spirit was also far more deeply rooted in general among us than among other nations, thanks to historical evolution, thanks to compulsory military service, which had long been in force, and to the German taste for outward show of strength. It is not to be wondered at that, under such circumstances, the heads of the Navy were sometimes tempted to shake off their dependence on the Foreign Office, and act independently, even despotically. For instance, on one occasion, the Admiralty took upon itself to call on the services of German consular representatives for strictly confidential matters, without first consulting the Foreign Office, and ascertaining whether there were any personal or other objections to this. In the matter of the new Nationality Law, the Bill was delayed for a long time by differences of opinion between the Foreign Office and the Navy, the latter thinking it knew more about the wishes and needs of Germans resident abroad than the central office for foreign affairs, which was relying on the long experience and opinion of its foreign representatives. The Navy wished to promote the spread of Germanism by giving them extensive exemption from patriotic duties, particularly from the obligation to serve in the Army. They were said to be sufficiently doing their duty to their country as pioneers of German commerce. The Foreign Office was of opinion that the Germans abroad ought to be given considerable relief in respect of military service, but not entirely absolved from the obligation. This would be an injustice to the Germans at home, and would have the effect of putting a premium on emigration. Experience taught that it was a good thing to strengthen, not to relax, the ties which bound Germans abroad to the mother country. The position taken up by the Admiralty was supported with such vigour, that the Imperial Chancellor, von Bethmann Hollweg, who had already had to deal with the matter as Home Secretary, was influenced by it. A fresh detailed enquiry into the disputed points, with the assistance of fresh expressions of opinion from our foreign representatives, was required, before the Chancellor could be brought round to the Foreign Office view, and the Bill finally shaped accordingly.

It is obvious that the disagreements between the Ministries were not calculated to further the management of foreign policy ; they were, on the contrary, productive of considerable difficulties and obstacles. This applied particularly to our relations with England, which were more and more clouded by our naval policy, and grew visibly darker. England, whose insular position and ramification over the world necessitated her maintaining a Navy of such strength as to be far superior to that of any other Naval Power, was very much perturbed by our naval projects, and the sensational way in which they were being pushed forward. At first it was probably thought that our programme of naval construction would not be carried out in full

When this hope proved delusive, counter measures were taken, first to assemble a fleet of considerable strength in the North Sea, thus presenting a front against us, then to outbid us by constructing new giant battleships—Dreadnoughts—and finally efforts were made to intimidate us. A chorus of noisy Press voices resounded from the other side of the North Sea, and here and there an insolent threatening speech from a responsible quarter. The result was merely to strengthen our resistance, and thus intensify the antagonism. The idea now suggested itself, at first tentatively, then more forcibly, of trying to settle the matter amicably. English statesmen advocated a general *rapprochement,* and even went so far as to propose an alliance, but this did not inspire our Government with the degree of confidence in its stability which would have been necessary to justify a change in our policy.

The first serious step taken in the direction of limiting naval construction, apart from an unsuccessful effort made at the second Hague Conference, was on the occasion of a meeting between the Kaiser and King Edward at Homburg. The King, however, was cautious enough to leave the Under-Secretary of State, Sir Charles Hardinge, who accompanied him, to act as principal in the negotiations No discussion of naval questions took place between the two Monarchs. Hardinge made suggestions to the Kaiser which practically amounted to a proposal that we should cut down our ship-building programme, without anything more than an indefinite prospect being held out of England's doing the same. The Kaiser made it perfectly clear that an understanding on such a one-sided basis was out of the question, and was very short with Hardinge when he remarked that in that case England would be compelled to emphasise her superiority more strongly.

The relations soon became strained to such a degree that public opinion on both sides grew apprehensive, and efforts to create a more friendly atmosphere were made, in the form of reciprocal visits from Press representatives, mayors, and clergy. The visits, accompanied by many pretty speeches, went off very satisfactorily, but the good impression made failed to remove the main causes of the strained relations.

The future now looked so dark that the Government made an effort to relieve the tension. Prince Bülow personally thought it advisable that more prominence should be given to the defensive character of German naval armament, possibly by paying more attention to submarines, coast defences, and mines, but his wish did not prevail against the advocates of building battleships. Consequently, there was no course open except to arrive at an understanding as to the naval programme. The possibilities were limited, owing to our being tied by the Naval Bill The utmost that could be done would be to reduce the pace at which new ships were being laid down, allay suspicion by giving the English free insight into what was going on in our dockyards, and consider the question of abandoning any further increase in our Navy in the distant future. In return for such limitation of our power, it was hoped that England would enter into a treaty of neutrality, an idea with which I did not personally associate myself, as it seemed to me hopeless

It was not without difficulty that the consent of the Admiralty to these plans was secured Admiral von Tirpitz obstinately opposed far-reaching demands made by the Chancellor, and repeatedly weighed down the scale heavily, by threatening to resign.   Our conferences with the English states- men, which were at first quite confidential and un- official, were not unpromising in the beginning, but they finally ended in smoke, when it became evident that our proposals did not satisfy the English.   We never got so far as to discuss the idea of neutrality.

The new Chancellor, von Bethmann Hollweg, who looked on improving our relations to England as one of his most important and urgent duties, made a fresh effort to lessen the Anglo-German differences   It was now mainly a question of an understanding as to a fixed ratio in the number and type of big ships, in which we were prepared from the first to give England an advantage over us in proportion to her needs.   But again, on this occasion, the Conferences did not reach the point of starting formal negotiations, owing to the difficulty in fixing a ratio of ships which would correspond with the demands made by experts on both sides.   Thus this effort, too, fell through.   It was resumed later on, in conversations with Lord Haldane, at a time when I was no longer head of the Foreign Office, but it is well known that these discussions, in which we again gave prominence to our wish for a treaty of neutrality, did not lead to any satisfactory result.

Our Ambassador in London, Count Metternich,

a man of great merit, who thoroughly understood the English mentality, and had the valuable gift of far sight, had shown himself strongly in favour of a reasonable understanding with England. Admiral von Tirpitz was his resolute and pugnacious opponent. There were frequent sharp encounters between him and the Admiral at the preliminary Cabinet Councils, which Count Metternich was requested to attend. I always took the part of the single-minded Ambassador, of whom the Kaiser also had a very high opinion at first. Later on, after my time at the Foreign Office, the antagonism became so pronounced as to prejudice the position of our representative in London, and lead to his place being taken by Freiherr von Marschall.

There was also a difference of opinion with regard to Eastern Asiatic policy. Our Kiau-Chow territory was administered by the Admiralty, which had done admirable and most promising work there in a short time, and wanted to do more in the same direction. Admiral von Tirpitz was anxious that the German troops which had been in China since the Boxer expedition should be transferred to Tsingtau, when they were no longer needed, in order to make it a first-class fortress. This scheme was frustrated by the troops being ordered home at the request of the Foreign Office, which urged important political reasons for their recall. To-day there can be no doubt as to which side was right.

The work of drawing up a declaration of maritime law in London, as a result of the second Hague Conference, was also going on during my early days of office. Almost all our proposals were successfully carried through, and a substantial improvement in maritime law was consequently achieved, in the sense of greater safeguards being provided for commercial freedom and private property. The English representatives signed the draft of the Declaration with the others, but although the British Government did not explicitly refuse to ratify it, they continually delayed the ratification. Their hands were therefore freer in this direction in the World War, and they made the well-known disastrous use of the freedom. The incident throws a significant light on English statesmanship, which is fond of arraying itself in the garb of humanity and justice.

My début in the Reichstag, which of course I did not look forward to without trepidation, was not made under very happy auspices. I had been ill not long before, and still felt very limp, but as it was a question of the Foreign Office Budget, I wanted to be in my place. In addition to this, there was an unexpected *contretemps* on the day itself. The House was well filled, but the journalists' benches were empty. The press representatives had taken serious · umbrage at very unparliamentary language a Centrum deputy had used to them at the previous sitting, and were on strike. Under these inopportune circumstances, Prince Bulow avoided speaking, but I could not back out of the obligation. In the end I got on better than I expected. My statements, which concerned Morocco, the Anglo-Russian agreement with regard to Asia, the Bagdad railway, the Baltic and North Sea agreements, and a few trifling matters, were well received   On this first occasion I had prepared my speech.   Later, in the case of questions which could not be foreseen, this was not feasible. But I also got on quite well, speaking on the spur of the moment, and I found that the deputies preferred this, on account of the speeches being more spirited, and confined to the main points.   If it so happened that I had not time to go very deeply into a matter, or so much was at stake that every word had to be carefully weighed beforehand, I got out of the difficulty by reading a statement or explanation here and there.   That always left an unfavourable impression.

Thanks to the Reichstag being in a good humour, the Budget debate went off absolutely without a hitch, so much so that one or two things the Budget Committee had struck out were reinserted by the Plenum.   It is true that the Reichstag withdrew these concessions on the third reading, solely, as the well-meaning mover of the proposal informed me in confidence, on the fixed principle of not giving the Government all it asked.

The incorporation of Bosnia and Herzegovina in the Habsburg monarchy, proclaimed on October 8, 1908, ushered in a period full of anxiety and unrest. It has often been stated in public that this event took the German Government completely by surprise.   That is quite a fallacy.   It was obvious that the rivalry between Russia and Austria-Hungary, who were now contending for the upper hand in the Balkans, instead of pursuing the policy agreed on at Murzteg, must lead to the Balkan question being more or less forcibly solved , equally obvious that the first important step would be taken by the Danube monarchy, which was eagerly competing for expansion of power under Baron Aehrenthal's guidance, not from Russia, who was still disabled.

It is true that it was not clear at first what the step would be, and when it would be taken.. Nevertheless, the constitutional upheaval in Turkey, and the question it raised whether elections were also to be held in the provinces of Bosnia and Herzegovina, which were legally under the jurisdiction of Austria-Hungary, according to the Berlin Congress, although nominally still under the sovereignty of the Sultan, foreshadowed some unusual event. Moreover, a month before the announcement of the annexation, Baron Aehrenthal had made a point of acquainting me with his plans, on the occasion of a visit he paid me at my country place in Bavaria, where I was spending my leave. The proclamation was to be made " at the given moment." He could not yet decide the exact moment, as it still depended on various circumstances. He did not expect any very great opposition on the part either of Turkey or Russia. He proposed to settle the matter satisfactorily with Turkey by letting her have the Sanjak, which it would be very difficult to hold by military force in case of any armed conflict ; he did not anticipate any serious difficulties with Russia, all the less as she was incapable of action for the present. " The Bear will growl and snarl, but won't bite or strike out with its claws." In reality, none of the European Powers had any good reason for interfering, for it was not a question of an actual change in the existing position, merely of a formal change Serbia would cry out, certainly, as a great obstacle would have been thrown in the way of her fine schemes. " Then she will just have to put up with the consequences of her attitude " This remark threw a light on the deeper motives which prompted the step. It was less a question of adding to the lustre of the Habsburg crown, or of evading the difficulty as to the Turkish elections, than of setting a *rocher de bronze* in the way of the Pan-Serbian undermining work, which was being actively carried on, with Russian assistance, in the south-eastern portions of the Monarchy.

In answer to Baron Aehrenthal's question as to what I thought of his plan, and whether he could count on our support, I said that I could not altogether share his view that there would be no hitch. Comparatively recent experience in the matter of the Sanjak railway showed that a group of Powers existed, to whom any excuse for taking the strongest measures to prevent Austro-Hungarian influence from making headway in the Balkan provinces would be welcome. I agreed that the " Russian bear would not bite," but it would certainly do all it could to create difficulties. As far as the attitude of the German Government was concerned, I could only say, for the present, that its fixed principle was to further the interests, wishes and requirements of its ally in the matter of the Balkans. But the idea of employing armed force against Serbia in case of need, seemed to me very extravagant.

Baron Aehrenthal had already uttered similar threats against Serbia in an earlier conversation with me, on the occasion of the Kaiser's visit to the Emperor Francis Joseph, at Schonbrunn, in the spring, with the heads of the German Federal States, and I had not concealed from him that high-handed procedure might have far-reaching and serious consequences. As to the date of proclaiming the annexation, I imagine that Baron Aehrenthal wanted first to secure a further means of putting pressure on Serbia, by drawing Bulgaria into the orbit of Vienna policy. The declaration of Bulgaria's independence, which was made at the same time as the annexation, confirmed this view.

The minor crisis over the Sanjak railway, which occurred a few months before the Bosnian crisis, was brought about by Baron Aehrenthal's having publicly propounded a scheme to carry on the construction of the Bosnian railway in the direction of Salonica, on the ground of the rights conceded to the monarchy at the Berlin Congress. Although Austria-Hungary's right to do this was incontestable, and the economic value of the undertaking obvious, most of the Powers were furious, and a violent outcry was raised in the Press, led by the English Press. Not only Russia, France, and England, but also Italy, and particularly Serbia, protested strongly against the railway project, to which they imputed political rather than economic aims. They may have been right in this view, in so far as the economic expansion of the Danube Monarchy towards the southern 'Balkans could but increase its power, and must at the same time have the effect of sensibly interfering with the Pan-Serbian schemes of expansion. The Powers named therefore agreed upon a counter-move, the project of a railway which should link up the Danube with the Adriatic. We adopted the standpoint of recognising the cultural and economic importance of the Sanjak railway undertaking from the first. In reality, laying railway lines in the disturbed parts of the Turkish Empire was calculated to do more than anything else to show the antagonistic peoples that there was more to be gained by opening up the country to profitable economic activity, than by sanguinary strife and the tutelage of Powers who forced unsuitable reforms on them. The question of railway construction was still under consideration, when it was overtaken by the proclamation of the annexation. It had been, as it were, the prelude to this event, and had had the one advantage of showing Austro-Hungarian diplomacy how strongly attempts to make headway in the Balkans would be opposed.

Baron Aehrenthal's bold step was unwelcome to us, in so far as it was likely to lead to complications, and intensify the existing antagonisms. There was no reason to suppose, in the first instance, that the complications would become such as to involve the serious risk of war, but at the same time we had to reckon with this remote possibility. On the other hand, our own interests, far more than the obligations of our alliance—for this only applied to the case of a Russian attack—demanded that we should stand by our Ally as a matter of course, and back her up strongly in resisting any attempt to undermine her position as a great Power. For it was only as a great Power that our Ally was of value to us, both as the guardian of European peace, and also as a sentinel on the routes to the East, where a wide field of economic expansion was open to us. If we left Austria-Hungary to depend on herself at a critical moment, which might decide not only her fate but our own, there was a risk of her strength not being equal to the onslaught, and of her joining our enemies in order to save her own existence.   Our help could, moreover, only be effective if it made its influence, clearly and distinctly felt. We therefore not only consented to the step, but promised our loyal support.

Before the announcement of the annexation it had already become evident that Russia would make difficulties. As a matter of fact, M. Isvolsky had also paid me a visit, shortly after having had a meeting with Baron Aehrenthal and the Ambassador, Count Berchtold, at Buchlau, the residence of the latter. There he was frankly told of the proposed annexation, and in return for his consent a prospect was held out that Austria-Hungary would agree to the Dardanelles being opened in favour of Russia. M. Isvolsky seemed far from satisfied with the conversation at Buchlau. He spoke in a tone of irritation of Aehrenthal's adventurous schemes, which he put down to personal ambition. He pointed to the necessity for solving the questions they raised at a Conference, if not a Congress, and hinted that if we stood by our Ally he would be obliged to lean more on the Western Powers than he wished. I evaded his repeated efforts to obtain enlightenment in this direction by pointing out that this was a question of such importance that I could not say anything without the authority of the Chancellor. At the same time I left him to draw his own conclusion, from the logic of the general position, as to the side on which

6

our interests lay He then went to London and
Paris, but there he apparently secured agreement
to oppose the annexation schemes, but no definite
promise as to the degree of support that would
be forthcoming, and, above all, found no inclination
to solve the Dardanelles question in the Russian
sense.

I knew, from having been his colleague in Copenhagen, what M. Isvolsky thought as to this. His
idea was that the Straits should be open to Russian
ships, but not to the ships of other nations. Thus
the fortified Straits were to be a sally-port for
Russia, a barricade to the others; the Turkish
fortresses were to be of service to Russia, and, if
possible, with the help of German material and
German leaders. From London and Paris M.
Isvolsky came to Berlin, the annexation having
already taken place, with a view to making fresh
efforts there to induce us to withdraw from our Ally.
This was all the less successful, as he had nothing
to offer us, and even had to half admit that he
had not obtained what he hoped from the Western
Powers. Having personally been treated in an unfriendly manner in the highest quarter, over and
above the political rebuff, he started on the return
journey to Russia in a very bad temper.

The crisis ended, as is well known, in Russia,
and the Powers which sided with her, demanding
that the matter should be dealt with at a Conference, as things which meant an alteration of what
had been agreed on at the Berlin Congress could
only be settled by the Powers jointly. The Vienna
Government did not at all favour the idea of a
Conference. Our suggestion that warning repre-

sentations should be made in Belgrade by all
the Powers found acceptance in London and Paris,
it is true, but was thwarted by separate action on
the part of the Russian Ambassador.   The difficulties of the position were increased by the fact
that Serbia did not confine herself to protests and
Press-warfare, but mobilised her army.   It was even
less possible for the Monarchy to yield to such
pressure than to the diplomatic pressure exercised
by the great Powers.   The idea which was mooted
of only summoning the Conference when agreement
had been reached between the Powers, consequently
for the purpose, as it were, of " registering "
the decisions, did not seem to us worth supporting, as this would have reduced the importance of
the Conference to a very low level, if not rendered
it altogether useless.

A moment came when it seemed likely that the
tension would last a long time, and that the complications would increase.   Prince Bulow was not
averse to letting things come to a climax, and to a
trial of strength between the Central Powers *bloc*
and the Triple Entente, which was not yet firmly
established, as he was convinced that none of the
Powers would draw the sword, and that, when it
came to a question of bending or breaking, Russia
would climb down from her high horse, and would
also call her vassal Serbia to order.   I shared his
confidence, but thought it advisable not to bend the
bow too tightly.   Unforeseen things might occur
which would resolve the diplomatic into an armed
conflict, and in view of the attitude of the Powers,
into a European war.   Under the existing circumstances, and in consideration of the stupendous

weapons of modern warfare, this would be a matter of appalling gravity and extent ; in addition to this, it would be a war for which our people would have neither sympathy nor enthusiasm. If Russia remained obdurate, relying on her own still considerable strength, and the support of her French ally and her new English friend, that would be a knot which could only be cut by the sword. If she yielded to our strong pressure, the fact of her doing so would amount to a defeat of the Russian Empire, and, particularly in view of M. Isvolsky's excessively sensitive and ambitious character, would have undesirable results ; in particular, that of welding the Entente all the more firmly against us. My opinion was that it would be advisable to act cautiously, while adhering firmly to the position we had taken up ; in this way we should avoid giving the impression of having been forced to relax the tension. Half the victory would have been won when we had convincingly shown that we were immovably loyal to our Ally, and were prepared to go to extremes in case of need. The best course now would be to turn our minds to solving the crisis by mediation. Prince Bulow was of the same opinion, and at a conference with the Kaiser, in which the Chief of the General Staff took part, it was decided to act accordingly.

As Russia's attitude was in reality inconsistent with promises she had made, even before the Berlin Congress, and she was now only clinging to the very weak point of a question of form, it might be assumed that she would welcome the prospect of an honourable retreat, all the more as she could hardly any longer fail to realise that neither of the

Powers to whom she had appealed for help was prepared to give more than diplomatic support. The solution we proposed was that each Power should give its consent to the annexation individually, consequently not at a Conference. This way out of the difficulty was facilitated by Serbia's having put her cause into the hands of the Powers, although it must be admitted that she did this in the belief that a Conference would take place

Everything now depended on whether Russia, whom we had to approach first, would accept our proposal. Fortunately, our representations in St. Petersburg were not unavailing ; the Russian Cabinet replied without hesitation in the affirmative. After this, the other Powers could not do otherwise than follow the Russian example, and thus the crisis was practically solved. The rest passed off without any difficulty. Serbia was induced to withdraw her protest and her demand for territorial compensation, and not only to demobilise, but to give a guarantee of good behaviour in future. The legend that our last communication to Russia was an ultimatum has been purposely circulated by our enemies. That is a deliberate misrepresentation of the facts. It must be admitted that our language in St. Petersburg was very forcible, as befitted the situation ; the preamble contained the phrase " in the event of the Russian Government not seeing its way to comply with our well-meant proposal, we should be obliged to leave things to take their course."

Although Europe was now relieved of a crushing anxiety, the political sky did not altogether clear. It was recognised that we had scored an important political success, and that the Triple Alliance had come triumphantly out of a trial of strength, and it was also impossible not to recognise that we had rendered a service to the cause of European peace, but dissatisfaction was felt at our having assumed the political leadership, and so strongly insisted on our position, that the tension had, after all, been in reality compulsorily relaxed. Our method of procedure and the tone we adopted left a painful impression in St. Petersburg for a long time, and a sting which roused a desire to retaliate, in spite of there being more cause there for thankfulness than for any other feeling.

Prince Bülow says in his book, *Deutsche Politik*, that after the Bosnian crisis normal relations were rapidly restored between us and Russia, as was proved by the satisfactory meeting between the emperors in the Finnish islands in the Baltic, in June 1909, and that the feeling in England had appreciably sobered down, as was shown by the harmonious way in which King Edward's visit to Berlin went off, " immediately after the turning-point of the crisis had been reached " ; but both statements must be accepted with reservations. It is true that when the Kaiser and the Tsar met again, the personal relations between the sovereigns were absolutely unaffected by what had occurred, and as cordial as before, but there could be no mistake as to the statesmen being in a very bad humour. Both M. Isvolsky and the Prime Minister, Stolypin, were influenced by a suspicion that, under Aehrenthal's leadership, Austria-Hungary might devise new schemes aimed against Serbia, and in that way against Russia too, and that she must

be feeling confident of our support. And, as far
as the English Royal visit is concerned, there is no
apparent connection between it and the solution of
the Bosnian crisis, for the visit took place on
February 9th, and the turning-point of the crisis,
i.e. Russia's answer agreeing to our proposal, was
not reached till March 26th.

In any case, later events showed clearly that
the encircling ring which had been drawn round
Germany had not by any means been broken up.
Two years later, in the summer of 1911, on the
occasion of the fresh Morocco crisis, England took
France's part against us with brutal distinctness, and
Russia had so little got over her diplomatic defeat
in 1909—as M. Isvolsky gave me to understand
later on in Paris—that she formed still closer
relations with France and England, and pushed on
her military preparations to an extent and in a way
which was an unpleasant surprise to us when the
World War broke out. Accordingly, there can be
no doubt that, although the Bosnian crisis was
peaceably solved, and through it we achieved a
great diplomatic success, it left a situation which
did not augur well for the future.

The attitude of our second Ally, Italy, during
the Bosnian crisis, was cautious, but on the whole
not unfriendly. It was not a case of another
" *extra-tour*," which is all the more deserving of
recognition, as Italy was confronted with a conflict
of interests not easy to solve. For some time past,
availing herself of the freedom of action the Triple
Alliance allowed its members, she had sought more
or less of a *rapprochement* to Russia, beginning
with a commercial treaty. Her taking this course

was accounted for by the fact that, in view of her interests in the territories on the far side of the Adriatic, Italy could not be indifferent to the growth of the Pan-Serbian movement, and thought she could best diminish the dangers of it by keeping on good terms with Russia, the protector of Slavdom, so as not to be elbowed aside in case of complications.

M Tittoni, the Italian Foreign Minister, who also came to stay with me at a time when the annexation of Bosnia and Herzegovina was not yet in sight, had explained this to me frankly. He assured me that Italy would loyally adhere to the Triple Alliance, which was of great value, if only because it was a sure guarantee that the Italians' passionate dislike of the Austrians would not become open enmity. It was true that Austria made the maintenance of friendly relations anything but easy, as she only turned a deaf ear to many reasonable Italian wishes. The Italian people were in sympathy with Germany, now as ever, although slight misunderstandings arose now and then, partly to be attributed to the personality of the German Ambassador in Rome, whose bad manner had made him disliked. Although Italy considerably strengthened her military position as against Austria in the course of the crisis, sharper conflict between the two associates in the Alliance was averted by pacifying influence on both sides. Not only during, but before and after the crisis, we always took pains to avert and tone down tension between Vienna and Rome. But obstacles were sometimes thrown in our way by others; for instance, the Tsar's visit to Racconigi, when the shorter route through

Austria was carefully and conspicuously avoided. It was a striking demonstration of the Russian policy which "employed the Italian counter-poison against the Austro-German bacillus."

The prospects of overcoming the Bosnian difficulty would have been still more gloomy, but for our having given timely consideration to the question of disposing, to some extent, of the anxieties our unsatisfactory relations with our Western neighbour caused us. France had not indeed taken up a strong attitude in the crisis, and evidently did not want the complications to be intensified to the point of war ; but she was among our enemies, and would not have stood aside in the long run, if it had come to that. Apart from the great question of Alsace-Lorraine, which, from our point of view, could not be raised, the differences between us and France were mainly in connection with Morocco. We had solemnly asseverated time after time that we were not pursuing any political aims there, or trying to gain a footing which would embarrass France in any way, we merely claimed the share in economic activity to which we were entitled. But this had not had the effect of smoothing away the points of friction ; public opinion in the two countries remained divided, and French distrust of us was still as strong as the tendency to interfere unwarrantably in legitimate German proceedings. If we did not wish to be involved in fresh serious conflict on account of Morocco—and no sensible German could wish this— the only thing was to try to put an end to the doubts which were perpetually arising as to what the one or the other or both were entitled to do, by making this clearer, in short, by an understanding as to the limits to be observed. If such an understanding could lead to an *entente* in matters which were not in dispute, so much the better. I already had visions of something of this kind, when the disturbances in Morocco, in the summer of 1908, created a fresh difficult situation. It would have been more serious, but for my having dealt with the burning question of recognising the successful aspirant to the throne, Mulai Hafid, in such a way as to make our intention of supporting the new Sultan perfectly clear, and at the same time deprive France of any grievance.

The Casablanca incident was an unforeseen obstacle in the way of further progress. Our German consular representative there had helped not only German, but other foreign legionaries to escape, in an apparently unwarrantable way; French military police had intervened, and there had been serious fighting. At first it was not quite clear, from the scanty material to hand, which side was most to blame. Each naturally tried to exonerate itself, and put the blame on the other, even more in the Press, which got hold of the affair at once, and in Paris and London, where fuel was added to the flame by asserting that the whole thing was manœuvred from Berlin in order to raise fresh strife over the heated Morocco question, than in the official reports. English influence in Paris also did a good deal of harm. The French were given to understand that a favourable opportunity had arrived for a reckoning with Germany, who would have to stand alone against France, Russia, and England, as Austria-Hungary was still hampered by the Bosnian crisis. There would be no difficulty in restraining Italy. The impression made by these English suggestions was not clearly recognised at that time, still, much could be read between the lines of Press utterances, which led to the conclusion that the fuel which kept the flames alight in Paris was not altogether a home product. As far as we were in a position to judge, the French had been far more to blame in the fighting than the Germans. There seemed no doubt that if the consulate had not been actually attacked, the consul's exceptional position had been disregarded. On the other hand, it could not be said that the Germans were in no way to blame.

The legal questions were more complicated, the question of whether, and how far, the consul was entitled to afford protection and help to deserters, and, on the other hand, the question of whether, and how far, French officials were entitled to make the protection illusory. There were strong differences of opinion as to this. We insisted that the German consul was not only entitled, but that it was his duty, to help Germans who appealed to him for protection as far as he possibly could.

The question of what had actually occurred was also disputed ; the French declared that the German statement of the facts, which we had brought to their notice without delay, was not exhaustive, and was in many respects incorrect. At first, however, no counter-evidence was brought forward. A proposal that the matter should be settled by both parties stating that they regretted the mistakes made by their official representatives, having been rejected, I suggested, on my own initiative, that the vexed questions should be submitted to arbitration. How M. Clemenceau, the then Prime Minister, could have asserted, as he so repeatedly did in public, that it was he who made the proposal of arbitration, and that we had rejected it, passes comprehension. Anyhow, my suggestion proved useful ; the French Government hastened to adopt it, the excitement in Paris and London died down quickly, and the matter would have been satisfactorily settled without further disagreement, had not differences of opinion arisen as to the questions to be submitted to the Court of Arbitration

One of the drawbacks to the settlement of disputed points by arbitration is that it sometimes raises fresh and more serious questions than the main question   The standpoint we upheld was that the Court of Arbitration should only be competent to solve the theoretically legal questions , we had no reason for questioning the facts, for the time being, as we had not received a detailed French statement.   The French, however, wished both questions dealt with, the question of facts as well as the legal question.   This involved fresh negotiations and fresh irritation.   A suspicion gained ground in Paris that we were trying to back out of the arbitration, lest it should be to our disadvantage.   Newspaper articles, emanating from German National circles, which opposed the idea of arbitration, strengthened this impression   The Chancellor considered whether pressure should not be exercised in order to secure agreement to our proposal, a step from which I dissuaded him, as it would only have added to the difficulties   To all appearance it was a case of fresh misunderstandings. Pressure would not help to remove them. The Crown Prince also interfered in the matter by urging stronger action. Added to all this I was suddenly taken seriously ill Before I had recovered from this illness, the French official report on the fighting came to hand. It was far more detailed than ours, and made very serious charges against our consular officials, innumerable depositions of witnesses being appended. There seemed to me no doubt that under these circumstances, which shook the view hitherto held, we could not refuse to do justice to the French wish that the question of facts should be submitted to arbitration, as well as the legal question. In spite of my being ill, I went to see the Chancellor, and he quite agreed with me. A few days afterwards, Herr von Kiderlen having temporarily taken my place at the Foreign Office, the understanding as to the duties of the Court of Arbitration was reached.

The Solomon-like verdict given by the Court, after a considerable lapse of time, had a pacifying effect on the whole, although it did not give universal satisfaction. In substance it was almost identical with the proposal we had made in Paris, and which was rejected—mistakes on both sides, mutual regrets. True, it made a painful impression on those of my fellow countrymen who favoured a sabre-rattling policy, and there were many who thought I had been more accommodating than was advisable. But these adverse criticisms did not alter my view that we ought to adhere to the policy of smoothing over differences with France, particularly in view of the tension caused by the Bosnian crisis. At a time when all our diplomatic skill was needed in the East, it seemed very necessary that we should not be hampered with difficulties in the West. France's comparatively passive attitude during the Bosnian crisis was encouraging in this respect. The Chancellor and the Kaiser entirely agreed. Consequently I resumed the idea of a Morocco agreement, which had already been mentioned to the French Ambassador. At the Chancellor's wish I left Herr von Kiderlen, who, after having acted for me, still remained in the office as an assistant, to carry through a programme I had drawn up with him. The negotiations made rapid and satisfactory progress. Only one difficulty arose, and this I was able to overcome, in connection with my earlier conversations with the French Ambassador.

On February 9, 1909, the agreement was signed by me and the Ambassador, M. Jules Cambon. It confirmed the Algeciras Acts, laid stress on the integrity and independence of the Shereefian Empire, and underlined economic equality of right. It stated that Germany only pursued economic aims, and recognised France's special political interests. Besides this, it proposed combined economic action by the subjects of the two States. The agreement was welcomed on all sides, and certainly with justice, as a means of escape from an unpleasant and somewhat dangerous position We gave up no rights, no interests, and no hope, as we were here and there said to have done It had already been stated at Algeciras that we did not want to play any political part in Morocco ; the way was now paved, and good prospects opened up for our

economic activities. The chief value of the agreement, however, lay in the proof that an understanding was possible between the two nations in a
restricted area, which excluded any possibility, of
strife and conflict as long as both sides honestly
and sincerely wished to observe it loyally. We,
for our part, have certainly not failed in this.

A curious chance decreed that the agreement
should not be signed at the hour fixed for this,
and for the public announcements which had been
prepared M. Jules Cambon, who had gone to Paris
to obtain the consent of the Government in person,
did not turn up at the appointed time. His train
was several hours late, as it had to pull up to allow
the special train conveying the King of England
to Berlin, to pass. It was not until I returned
from King Edward's formal reception that M.
Cambon and I met to sign the agreement, he in
travelling clothes and I in full uniform.

The incorporation of the nominally still Turkish
provinces of Bosnia and Herzegovina, and the
attitude we adopted towards this event, had not only
led to tension between the Powers, but had the
unpleasant additional effect of temporarily calling
our friendly relations with Turkey in question. We
were in reality, the Power which most sincerely, acted
on the fixed principle of maintaining Turkey's unimpaired territorial position. Our commercial
activity, both in European and in Asiatic Turkey,
with its rich prospects, necessitated our adopting
the attitude of a friend and protector. Turkey
appreciated this all the more as the Ottoman Empire
itself derived considerable and increasing advantages from our activity, and noted with satisfac-

tion how her latent energies were roused under our guidance.

In addition to the value of our economic and cultural influence, the military instruction we were giving, with obviously good results, was a further consideration The other Powers also inscribed maintenance of the *status quo* on their banners, but with few exceptions every thinking man in Turkey was fully aware that the most selfish con-siderations, and the hope of being able to shatter and dismember the Empire and gather in rich spoils, lurked beneath this superscription. Conse-quently, they rightly distrusted the ever-renewed attempts to force doubtful reforms on them, and had the strength of mind to oppose them obstinately. We always adopted a very cautious attitude towards these questions of reform, and refused to support some which were entirely unsuitable, such as the question of judicial reform. Neither did we take any part in the administrative reforms which England and Russia carried out in Macedonia, with the unmistakable intention of cutting off this district from the Turkish Empire

Events soon showed how justifiable this caution was, for there is no doubt that this scheme of reform, agreed upon at Reval, was responsible for the constitutional upheaval in Turkey, in which a hitherto unknown spirit of national self-reliance played an active part, under the leadership of the Young Turk Party The new régime began by showing us some coldness, in the belief that the position we had held in Turkey was only based on the friendly personal relations between the Kaiser and the Sultan, and that the Conservative character of our political life would not be well-disposed towards the advanced Liberalism which now had the upper hand in Constantinople. It was soon recognised that this was a mistake, and then the Young Turks became most friendly to us. The annexation of Bosnia and Herzegovina seemed likely to have the effect of clouding the excellent relations which had been restored, in so far as Constantinople, influenced from outside, suspected us of having egged on Austria-Hungary. But even this suspicion was dispelled by the facts, and by our unfailing friendliness to Turkey. And when it became known that we were trying to persuade the Vienna Government to soothe Turkey's injured *amour propre* by evacuating the Sanjak, the former friendly relations were restored. Since then they have left nothing to be desired.

Not only was the difficulty of the general situation in Europe aggravated by the Bosnian affair, but in spite of all our friendliness to the United States of America, as shown for instance in Prince Henry of Prussia's visit, and the interchange of professors, a slight cooling off in our relations with the great Power across the ocean could not escape the notice of an attentive observer, although it was so slight as to be scarcely perceptible. It was mainly caused by difficulties in connection with our reciprocal protectionist policy, a sphere not easily accessible to diplomatic influence. The strong influence of the English Press, which invariably worked against us, and with large resources, was also increasingly evident over there. For instance, efforts were made to saddle us with responsibility for the failure of a general Arbitration Treaty with

7

the United States, the truth being that a treaty, which had already been concluded was rejected by the American Senate, and a fresh proposal was of such a character that even with the best will —and this was not lacking on our part—it could no more be adapted to our constitutional institutions than our legitimate wishes could count on fulfilment, in view of the American political position.

Another incident, which concerned the appointment of a successor to the American Ambassador, Mr. Charlemagne Tower, also influenced feeling over there temporarily. The Foreign Office had been advised by our Ambassador in Washington— before I entered on office—that President Roosevelt intended to make personal changes in several ambassadorial posts. He thought of appointing Mr. David Jayne Hill, the Minister in the Netherlands, to Berlin The reply sent to the Ambassador was that Mr. Hill would be well received in Berlin if the President's choice should fall on him. There are well-known formalities to be observed in requesting and granting the *agréments,* usual in diplomatic intercourse, and we did not consider this communication anything more than a feeler, which would be followed in due course by a formal request for the *agréments.* Many months elapsed, however, without anything further being done in the matter, so that there was some justification for doubting whether President Roosevelt was still of the same mind. Mr. Tower, who had continued to act in Berlin, shared this doubt, all the more as he had not received any official intimation of a proposed change. In the meantime it had been concluded, from the fact that the lease of the house occupied by the Ambassador was not renewed, that the presumable successor was not in an equally favourable financial position. People in Berlin began talking of its being difficult for Mr. Hill, in case he were the successor, to adapt his mode of living even approximately to that of the other accredited representatives of the great Powers in Berlin, and concluded from the long delay in making the change that Mr. Hill himself hesitated to accept the post.

On the occasion of an entertainment given by Mr. Tower, who was presumably soon leaving, he spoke of these difficulties to the Kaiser, and said he thought President Roosevelt, who still seemed not to have come to any definite conclusion with regard to his successor in Berlin, would certainly be very willing to send some one who would be specially suitable for Berlin, if he heard that the Kaiser wished this. The American Ambassador in Rome, Mr Griscomb, who was present at the entertainment with his wife, would be just the right man, and would consider himself fortunate if he were appointed to fill the vacancy. He, Mr. Tower, would willingly make a suggestion to that effect in strict confidence to President Roosevelt if he had the Kaiser's authority for this. The Kaiser asked me how matters stood with regard to the *agrément* for Mr. Hill. I replied that Mr. Hill had been spoken of some months before, the Kaiser had at that time sent word that he would be welcome, but nothing had since been heard of the matter, no request had yet been made for *agréments* in the usual way. The Kaiser then signified his approval of Mr. Tower's proposal.

To our surprise difficulties arose in the way of Mr Tower's suggestion in Washington ; first the American, then the English Press, got hold of the story, and what had occurred was incorrectly reported as having been that the Kaiser had rejected Mr. Hill, because he was not sufficiently well off. The result was a violent agitation in the Press, which could only be silenced with difficulty, and with Mr. Tower's kind help. Even in the Reichstag circles there was some uneasiness. People talked of personal régime, and were on the point of setting the important machinery of an interpellation in motion.

In reality there was no occasion for such excitement. Although the incident was unfortunate, there could be no question of a serious offence against rules and customs It is by no means an unusual thing for one side to express a wish that a particular person should be sent who would be a specially welcome representative, and for the other willingly to agree to this, and it has often happened in the history of diplomacy. Later on, when Mr. Hill entered on his new duties, he was cordially received by the Kaiser, and by official and unofficial society in Berlin, and that ended the matter When our Ambassador, Freiherr Speck von Sternburg, died in Washington soon afterwards, President Roosevelt was privately given an opportunity of selecting from three candidates for the post, the one he would prefer. The answer was not quite definite, but suggested that Count Bernstorff would be particularly welcome. The *agrément* was then requested and granted. If a trace of annoyance still remained from the Hill case, this, at all events, put an end to it. In the purely political sphere, the fact that we agreed with America in recognising and acting on the principle of the open door in China, gave great satisfaction.

The Hill case had been preceded by another, which had equally given rise to complaints of personal régime, and had led to a debate in the Reichstag. It was a question of a private letter from the Kaiser to the English First Lord of the Admiralty, Lord Tweedmouth, in which some statistical and other particulars as to our Navy were given, in connection with former conversations, in order to do away with prejudices, and correct actual mistakes. The fact of the letter, rather than its purport, had become known through a blunder on the part of Lord Tweedmouth, and there was violent excitement in England as well as in Germany over the Kaiser's personal interference, and alleged unconstitutional procedure. The Chancellor defended the Kaiser in the Reichstag. In doing so, however, he made no reference to a not unimportant circumstance, the fact that the Kaiser had shown me the letter before sending it. I had not seen any reason for dissuading him from sending it Why should he not be at liberty to carry on by letter a useful conversation he had begun by word of mouth? Were not other Sovereigns in the habit of taking liberal advantage of similar freedom, and, as is well known, making far less well-intentioned and harmless use of it. Satisfaction in giving the English Minister fresh proof of the superiority of his expert knowledge may, to a certain extent, have influenced the Kaiser, but that makes no difference to the harmlessness of the correspondence.

An incident of greater importance, again a question of the Kaiser's sayings and doings, and their painful consequences, was the *Daily Telegraph* affair, the publication by this English newspaper of conversations with the Kaiser, and the circulation of the publication, apparently semi-officially. I had personally very little to do with this extremely painful matter, as the misunderstanding in the Foreign Office, which was responsible for the misfortune, occurred at a time when I was absent. What I know from my own experience of this matter, which has still never been fully explained in public, is as follows :—

On October 11, 1908, at seven o'clock in the evening, the Imperial Chancellor sent to ask me to come to his house for a discussion of the position created by the incorporation of Bosnia and Herzegovina in the Habsburg Monarchy. The official quarter whence this message was passed on to me —here the i's must be dotted—sent me at the same time an insignificant-looking document in a closed portfolio, with a remark that it was a private matter ; the Chancellor had said that he would look into it himself, but he had not done so yet, although it seemed urgent. I had no time to read the document, as I had to obey the Chancellor's summons to a conference at once, but a glance at the outside sheet showed me that it was the draft of a letter beginning " My dear Martin " ! Martin was Prince Bülow's cousin, von Jenisch, the Minister who was then with the Kaiser at Rominten as the Foreign Office representative. The draft was in the handwriting of von Müller, the Minister who had been acting as the Chancellor's Secretary at Nordeney till the day before. After the discussion of the Bosnian question, which lasted a long time, I gave Prince Bülow the document, remarking that it had been handed to me when leaving my office, and that I had not had time to look into it. The Chancellor took the document, and, after glancing at it casually, said it was a matter which had been attended to, and had now only to be signed. He said nothing as to the purport of the document, nor did he read it in my presence. It should further be noted that the Kaiser had lunched with the Chancellor that day, Prince Bulow having arrived from Nordeney in the morning. After lunch the Kaiser had a long talk with the Chancellor, in the garden, at which I was not present. On this occasion, as I gathered from something the Kaiser said later on, the question of publishing the document was discussed. The Kaiser asked that the matter should be finally settled, and the Chancellor gave his consent to the publication.

Rather more than a fortnight later, towards 10 a.m. on October 28th, the Chief of the Press Department, Councillor Hamman, sent me a very illegible copy of an article published by the *Daily Telegraph,* on conversations the Kaiser was said to have held. It had been submitted to him by Wolff's Bureau with the enquiry, usual in matters of importance, whether it might be circulated. As I came across several doubtful passages in reading the rendering of the conversations, I wrote a large and distinct " No " in red pencil on the enquiry form, and had the papers returned to the Wolff Bureau at once. At midday Councillor Hamman called on me, and said it did not seem to him feasible to prevent the circulation by Wolff. This would not avail to avert the commotion the *Daily Telegraph* article would cause, and would only give rise to all sorts of misunderstandings, as people would come to know of the article through other channels. As to that, a Berlin midday paper had already given extracts from it. As neither I nor Hamman knew anything of the original history of the article, I asked him to find out what the Foreign Office knew about it from Councillor Klehmet, who had to do with general political matters. Hamman returned in a few minutes with the amazing answer that the Kaiser and the Chancellor had agreed to its being published in an English paper some time ago. " If that is so," I said, " then I certainly have no further influence on the course of events." Thereupon the article was circulated by Wolff, consequently with, so to speak, the official *visa*—and the storm burst.

Subsequently I was able to ascertain how it all came about, almost without a break in the chain of evidence. The Kaiser's sayings had been put together by Colonel Stuart-Wortley, to whom he had expressed himself in the impulsive and frank way peculiar to him when he was staying at Highcliffe Castle, which had been rented for him from Colonel Stuart-Wortley, in the autumn of 1907. Colonel Stuart-Wortley thought he would be serving the interests of a better understanding between England and Germany by publishing what the Kaiser had said. From this point of view the Kaiser agreed to the publication, provided the Imperial Chancellor had no objection to it. The Kaiser had the draft sent him from England forwarded to the Chancellor, who was staying at Nordeney. Prince Bulow sent the manuscript to the Foreign Office, with instructions in his own handwriting to look through it and, after making any necessary erasures, alterations, or additions, to submit it to him again. The Under-Secretary, Stemrich, who was acting for me at that time, put the matter into Councillor Klehmet's hands, with the remark that it seemed to require special attention. Stemrich understood the Chancellor's instructions to mean that the Foreign Office was merely to enquire into whether, and how far, what the Kaiser had said was in accordance with what had actually taken place. After Klehmet had spent some days going through the manuscript, and had made some corrections, without talking it over, however, with any of the other Councillors or the Under-Secretary, as it was quite a private matter, it was returned to the Chancellor at Nordeney with a note stating that it had been dealt with according to instructions. There the matter seems to have rested for a few days, until the official document came into my hands for a passing moment, not long enough to enable me to master its contents, and then went back to the Chancellor.

The day after its publication, which made the greatest sensation, I had an opportunity of telling the Kaiser that, in consequence of an unfortunate misunderstanding, the draft of the *Daily Telegraph* article had not been dealt with as it should have been I had not had anything to do with it personally, but it was a question of the Government Office entrusted to me, and for whose proper management I was responsible. I must, therefore, ask him to accept my resignation. The Kaiser replied that there could be even less question of that than of the Chancellor's resignation, which he had just refused to accept. As to the rest, the thing would prove to be more harmless than it appeared at first sight. What he had said had been to some extent incorrectly rendered. For instance, he had not by any means forwarded an elaborate plan of campaign against the Boers to Windsor, but merely academic reflections in the form of aphorisms Moreover, he had spoken principally of facts which had long been public property.

A conference, in which Herr von Loebel, of the Chancellery, and Councillor Hamman also took part, was held the same day at the Chancellor's residence, to consider a semi-official statement for publication. I brought a draft with me, which spoke of a' most deplorable blunder, but avoided implicating the Foreign Office in any way. In addition to this I suggested the possibility of describing the statements as partially incorrect, with the consent of the author of the version given of the conversations. Prince Bülow, however, insisted on the Foreign Office being mentioned, otherwise all sorts of things would be assumed, and in the long run the office would necessarily have to be mentioned I could not persist in my opposition, but avoided expressly assenting to the wording of the announcement. To my surprise, the Chancellor asked me to tell Klehmet, whom he had taken to task very sharply the day before, that he would not suffer in any way.

The further proceedings, the heated debates in the Reichstag, the Kaiser's statement as to being

more careful in future, etc., are well known.   On
the evening of the day on which it was semi-
officially announced that a mistake had been made
in the Foreign Office, I was suddenly taken so
ill that I could not take any part in what followed.

After my return to work, I found the situation
changed in many ways.   The Chancellor's position
towards the Reichstag had been somewhat prejudiced, in spite of the statement the Kaiser had
been induced to make.   The way in which the
matter had been dealt with was felt by some to
have deplorably lowered the prestige of the Crown,
whilst others would have preferred still stronger
guarantees against the Kaiser's interfering personally in political matters.   The relations of confidence, it would not be too much to say of friendship, which had hitherto existed between the Kaiser
and the Chancellor, were also undoubtedly shaken
The Kaiser did not think enough had been done
to defend him.   The first time I had an opportunity
of meeting him again, on the occasion of the
Brazilian's Minister's first audience, I found him in
a very dejected frame of mind.   He only made a
few curt remarks on what had happened, and they
showed bitterness.   I heard from those about him
that he had been suffering from severe mental
depression, and that he had not quite got over it.
He still gave himself up to profound meditation,
and the idea was gaining ground that things were
not as they had been represented.   I avoided all
reference to the matter myself, all the more, as my
knowledge of the circumstances was only frag-
mentary at that time.   On our attending together
to report to the Kaiser, I was struck by his coldness

to the Chancellor, and he also gave up the visits to the Chancellor, which had been so frequent.

Months had gone by since the November explosion, when the Kaiser had a talk with me, shortly before his second visit to Corfu, and confided to me, with evident deep emotion, that he was now painfully convinced that the Chancellor not only had not defended him sufficiently, but had absolutely betrayed him. It was not a question of a mistake or of carelessness, but the Chancellor had purposely left the publication to take its course, counting on the affair ending in the Kaiser being subjected to a sort of mayor of the palace control. I was horrified, and implored the Kaiser to dismiss such evil thoughts from his mind. As far as I knew, there was nothing whatever to justify a belief which involved such a terrible accusation. I could not possibly concur in it. In spite of all I said, the Kaiser persisted in his view It was not based on indefinite suppositions, but on certainties. The Kaiser was also aware of the fact that at the stormy time when the incident was being publicly discussed by the German Ministers who had met in Berlin for a sitting of the Federal Council Foreign Affairs Committee, the idea of persuading him to abdicate had been under consideration The Kaiser had himself thought of abdicating at the time of his mental depression, but he resented the idea of its being urged on him.

The end of the November storm did not settle the matter as far as public opinion was concerned either. Many people were still asking whether it was only in the Foreign Office that a fatal blunder had been made, or whether mistakes might not have been made elsewhere too. They were looking for other culprits, and thought the Kaiser's travelling companion, the Minister von Jenisch, or the Chancellor's assistant at Nordeney, von Müller, might have been to blame. An injustice in both cases. Neither Jenisch nor Müller ever had occasion to express their own opinion on the subject matter of the conversations which were to be published, for, after the correspondence between the Kaiser and the Chancellor, which had been carried on through them, they would not have been justified in doubting that the draft had been examined in detail, and approved in the proper quarter. Both protested strongly against the attempt to make scapegoats of them. Muller, who was irascible, even threatened to make sensational revelations, a hint of which I took no notice, partly because I looked on it as the outcome of a passing fit of anger, partly, and chiefly, because I did not think it advisable to re-open the powder-barrel which had been closed with such difficulty.

The great change in the domestic political situation consequent on the fate of the great fiscal reform proposals, led to Prince Bülow's resignation. It is true that the *Daily Telegraph* incident played no small part in the matter, particularly as far as the Kaiser was concerned. The relations between the Kaiser and the Chancellor were and remained cool, and were confined to strictly conventional formalities, in strong contrast to what they had been formerly. To all appearance, the Kaiser had been firmly resolved to part with Bülow since the spring, but, much as it went against the grain with him, he thought it expedient, as a concession to Parliamentarism, not to let his going appear due to anything more than the domestic political situation. Consequently he postponed releasing him from office until the fiscal reform question was quite settled.

I had always got on well with the Prince, although the possibility of friction was very much favoured by the fact that, as a lifelong diplomat, and former Minister for Foreign Affairs, he was more closely connected with the Foreign Office than with any other Government Department, and that among his many activities, foreign policy was the sphere he preferred. In spite of this, however, Prince Bülow left me a far freer hand from the first than I had expected, or could claim. Our purely personal relations were excellent, thanks to the Prince's amiability, and thanks to the lavish hospitality he dispensed with the assistance of a charming and highly-gifted wife. The Chancellor also very willingly entrusted me with the duty of reporting to the Kaiser on current business, and, above all, he left personal questions in my hands.

Busy tongues said that Prince Bülow was rather jealous of the kind confidence the Kaiser showed in me. That is a foolish and petty misunderstanding of the facts and the characters. It was in the nature of things that differences of opinion should arise in the course of time, but they never went so far as to cause serious conflict, on the contrary they could always be easily overcome by frank discussion or by passing them over lightly. The *Daily Telegraph* affair was a case in point. I had been left quite out of account owing to my illness, and when the Prince subsequently asked my opinion, I frankly expressed doubt as to the matter having been properly dealt with as regards the Crown. After that we never discussed the subject again. We also differed occasionally as to the degree of influence to be conceded to the Reichstag. The Prince thought, for instance, that I went too far in giving the Committee detailed private explanations of proceedings in the Balkan crisis which were not generally known, and he also thought I did not oppose the deputies' anxiety to cut down administrative expenses as strongly as I ought, particularly in the matter of the Christmas gratuities to officials.

These Christmas gratuities were rather a delicate question. The custom had been introduced before my time, and was usual in other Ministries as well as in the Foreign Office. The abuse was merely that they were paid to a great extent out of funds which had been voted for other purposes. That was known to several deputies. They were therefore unquestionably within their legal rights in demanding their abolition. To have opposed them more strongly would have led to very painful discussions. As far as giving the Reichstag clearer insight into the workings of the political machine is concerned, my motive was the necessity of restoring confidence, which had been so severely shaken by the *Daily Telegraph* incident, that the work done in the Foreign Office served its purpose, and this result was achieved.

My place was taken during my illness by the Minister in Bucharest, von Kiderlen-Wächter, as the Under-Secretary, Stemrich, had also been obliged to take sick leave, on account of the serious state of his health. Herr von Kiderlen-Wächter was perfectly familiar with the business of the Foreign Office from former experience, and it may be as well to mention that he was sent for at my suggestion. He was generally looked upon in the Foreign Office as one of our most able diplomatic representatives, and that he had not risen to a higher position hitherto than that of Minister in Bucharest, was more due to extraneous circumstances than to any lack of appreciation of his valuable abilities. What singled him out as being specially suitable for the temporary management of the office was the fact of his being a specialist in Balkan questions, a particularly valuable qualification, in view of the Bosnian crisis. In the few weeks during which he acted as my deputy, he entirely justified all the hopes which had been fixed on him. His misadventure when he made his maiden speech in the Reichstag under peculiarly unfavourable circumstances, in the heat of the *Daily Telegraph* affair, does not detract from his merits.

Prince Bülow thought so highly of Kiderlen, that, in view of the doubt as to whether my health would allow of my resuming my duties, he contemplated proposing him as my successor. Apart from his political ability, he thought Kiderlen's strong personality and robust character would secure better results both at home and abroad than my more cautious and conciliatory nature. In the meantime the idea was not acted upon, as my health improved sufficiently to enable me to take over the work again. Besides this, the Prince's proposal to give me the ambassadorial post in Paris, for which he considered me specially suited, was frustrated

by Prince Radolin's indignant opposition.   I had
nothing whatever to do with this attempt, which
only came to my knowledge after its failure   Prince
Bulow then contented himself with proposing that
I should retain Herr von Kiderlen as assistant
till the Bosnian affair was settled.   I agreed to
this without hesitation, feeling confident that it
ought not to be difficult to avoid the unpleasantness which might arise from the fact that Kiderlen
was my senior in length of service, and was now
my subordinate with a prospect of succeeding me.
I was not disappointed in this hope.   I equally met
the Prince's wish that I should give Kiderlen an
opportunity of making up for his unfortunate début
in the Reichstag by taking a conspicuous part in
bringing about an understanding with France over
the Morocco affair.

On July 14, 1909, the former Home Secretary,
Herr von Bethmann Hollweg, was appointed successor to Prince Bulow.   Whether his predecessor
had urged him to make personal changes, and to
select Herr von Kiderlen as Secretary of State for
Foreign Affairs, and whether there may have been
difficulties in the way of carrying out this idea, as
was whispered here and there, I never knew.   I
had no occasion to enquire into the matter, as the
new Chancellor at once asked me to support him,
a mark of confidence I valued all the more as his
inexperience in matters of foreign policy gave my
position more weight than under Prince Bulow, a
trained diplomat.

Herr von Bethmann set zealously to work to
study current questions of foreign policy, and to
make himself thoroughly acquainted with the work-

8

ings of the Foreign Office, which was still under a cloud as a result of the *Daily Telegraph* incident, so that I was in constant communication with the new Chancellor. This soon gave rise to some misgivings in individual circles of public opinion, due to anxiety lest the Chancellor's dependence on my greater knowledge of the business might tempt me to pursue a policy of my own, which would not be a strong policy. What had led to this anxiety was, among other things, the fact that, in a confidential conversation with some Liberal deputies from Schlesvig, I had said that the struggle between Germans and Danes in our northern Mark, and indeed less the struggle itself than the way in which it was carried on, gave the Foreign Office no little trouble. This was in answer to certain questions arising out of a mistaken belief that negotiations were going on with the Danish Government. Something of what I had said leaked out, was misrepresented and misunderstood, and strengthened the belief which already existed in National circles that I might not be as firm in dealing with Danish wishes as was advisable.

Although this belief had so little foundation in fact, it made me even more careful than in Bülow's time to be guided by the Chancellor's wishes and instructions in all my political transactions. This was particularly the case with regard to purely Prussian affairs, in so far as it was possible to deal with them independently of the policy of the Empire, as I was less familiar with the Prussian psychology than the new Chancellor, who had been Prussian Prime Minister and Prussian Minister for Foreign Affairs. In this way I was able to

work on perfectly harmonious and friendly terms
with him.

The misgivings felt in strongly Nationalistic
circles as to my supposed tendency to be too complaisant in dealing with foreign countries, had
subsided, when a fresh Morocco question arose, and
the way in which it was handled revived and
accentuated these misgivings. It was a question
of the mining claims acquired by the firms of
Mannesmann Brothers in Morocco. The Foreign
Office had warmly supported the activity of these
enterprising pioneers of German peaceful penetration, so long as it was confined within the limits
of the legal position, which, it must be admitted,
was not very clearly defined. From the moment
when, in spite of our repeated warnings, these limits
were deliberately overstepped, the support had
necessarily to be withheld.

Much as it would have been in Germany's
interests that the so-called Mannesmann rights
should be recognised, and the deposits of ore in
Morocco exploited, we could not urge them with
the force we were asked to exert, because this
would have brought us into conflict with the
Moroccan political law formulated by all the Powers,
partly indeed on our initiative. In attempting to
insist on the view taken by Mannesmann Bros.
we should not only have been repudiating our own
signature, but we should have had to enter on a
struggle with an overwhelming majority of the
Powers—not with France alone, as was purposely
asserted—which would certainly have ended in a
diplomatic defeat. The only practicable way out of
the difficulty was for the different groups of interests

to come to an agreement amongst themselves, under the benevolent guidance of the Governments concerned.

France, whose interests were most in question, was prepared to agree to this on the basis of the Morocco agreement of February 1909 Later on the Mannesmanns were induced to take this course. We helped them with all the means at our disposal, and it was not the fault of the officials concerned that the results achieved were only shortlived. The question of the Mannesmann claims, which it was expected would be dealt with in the Reichstag, was thoroughly and comprehensively discussed, both from the legal, actual, and political point of view, by the Foreign Affairs Committee of the Federal Council, with the result that the view taken by the Foreign Office was unanimously approved by the members, as well as by the Imperial Chancellor.

The revival of the Federal Council Committee for Foreign Affairs, an institution provided for in the Constitution of the Empire, but which had not hitherto materialised, was a recent measure which would not have been achieved without my help. The oblivion into which this provision of the Constitution had fallen had long been noted with dissatisfaction in Bavaria and Wurtemberg, and repeated attempts had been made to repair the omission. These had been defeated in Berlin, however, where it was feared that the exercise of its functions by the Committee might lead to undesirable interference in the conduct of foreign policy, which pertained exclusively to the Imperial Government. I was, nevertheless, of the same opinion as the Chancellor—at that time still Prince Bulow—that the existence of the Committee could only tend to strengthen the federal character of the Empire, and that there would be no reason to fear its having a disturbing influence, if it were certain that the Committee would only exist for the purpose of enquiry. This certainty was acquired, and thus the Committee became an actual and valuable institution.

The controversy over the recognition and satisfaction of their claims was carried on by Messrs. Mannesmann with great heat, first of all in public, with the help of a powerful Press, and finally in the Reichstag, where it was discussed in detail in Committee, and then on broader lines in the Plenum. The result was that a large majority upheld the Foreign Office view. Messrs. Mannesmann then decided to adopt the course recommended by the Foreign Office of an understanding between the interested parties, but they first tried doing without official help. A private individual, the well-known Herr Walter Rathenau, offered to place his useful connections in Paris, and his business experience, at their disposal, in order to bring about the desired understanding, in the event of the Foreign Office giving him the necessary authority. I readily gave it, and as a matter of fact he did succeed in coming to an advantageous understanding in Paris, but having first agreed to it, Messrs. Mannesmann could not make up their minds to sign the agreement when it came to the point. Later on, as Ambassador in Paris, I resumed the efforts to reach an understanding on a fresh basis. I found the French Government, particularly the

Premier, M. Caillaux, very willing to help in the matter, and we were in so far successful, that the articles of agreement were signed in my study by the French parties concerned, and by Messrs. Mannesmann. The latter, however, backed out of the understanding in the further course of the negotiations. This failure made further official efforts out of the question.

The excitement caused by the Mannesmann affair was so great and so widespread that it led to an avalanche of the most violent attacks on the Foreign Office and its responsible head personally. Not only was it evident that these attacks were intended to undermine my position, but the intention was frequently plainly expressed. I had, to use a Bismarck expression, got into the "mud line," and was not only pelted with mud and stones, but also shot at with poisoned arrows, to an extent indeed which far exceeded the accepted limits of the extreme candour customary in political warfare.

I was frequently urged by friends to make a stronger stand against the spiteful attacks, whose inventions, misrepresentations, and base suspicions were inexhaustible. I only made up my mind to do this quite exceptionally, remembering that violent retaliation rarely leads to a satisfactory issue. Whenever I did turn upon one of my assailants, who had not taken refuge in anonymity, I invariably received the apologetic explanation that the attacks had been based on assumptions which it must now be admitted were mistaken. Equally this was generally followed by an assurance that nothing personal had been intended. Under such

circumstances, I did not feel it would be any
use pointing out the difference between what
was personal and what was objective.

The endless succession of attacks made on the
Foreign Office and its organs, in the Press and
in the Reichstag, which the instigators tried to
substantiate by recalling the *Daily Telegraph*
incident, and carelessness, mistakes, and inadequate
support of German interests in the Mannesmann
affair, ended without exception in the discom-
fiture of the attackers, so that confidence in
the office, which had been shaken, was restored.
There were unmistakable signs of a certain weari-
ness, a feeling indeed that the mark had been
overshot. The only result of a final effort made
by a specially intractable antagonist, who went
so far as to accuse me of " effeminacy," cring-
ing to foreign countries, and finally of untruth-
fulness, was to elicit an unusually sharp rebuff
from the Chancellor.

Before my term of office, the German people,
dissatisfied with the course of events, had already
begun to criticise foreign policy and those responsible for it, more than had been the custom
hitherto. At first it was very much a tentative
movement, groping in a fog without any definite
aim. People talked of mistakes of diplomacy,
without making it clear who or what was meant,
our foreign political statesmanship, the drift and
direction of our foreign policy, or the way in
which it was carried out by the foreign representatives, the " diplomats " ! When they thought
there was reason to find fault, the latter were
generally fixed upon, in the mistaken belief that

they were first and foremost to blame. This tendency to criticise them adversely was encouraged by the fact that, as Government servants, those blamed were not in a position to defend themselves, that they were not well known in their own country, and, in no small degree, by the fact that the feeling of the people in general was hostile to the diplomatic service. They still adhered to the exploded idea that a true diplomat was a polished society man; in the habit of concealing the truth beneath an insidious address and subtle phraseology. The very high position the representatives in foreign countries held also helped to rouse an unfriendly feeling.

A main cause of the prejudice was the atmosphere of mystery which surrounded diplomatic procedure. The less people were allowed to know, the more they were thrown on suppositions, on scanty explanations, or on the rare occasions on which the curtain was slightly raised, the greater the tendency to form opinions of persons and things based on insecure *points d'appui,* on deceptive appearances, and worthless externals. There was something to be said against almost every foreign representative—one devoted himself entirely to representation, another led the life of a hermit, this one showed too much, that one too little power of adapting himself to his surroundings, this one was too conciliatory, that one too harsh, and most of them were credited with owing their advancement to Court favour, or to their well-filled purses. The only ones in whom confidence was felt were those whose names were, rightly or wrongly, connected with some obvious success, no notice was taken of the ones who toiled un-ostentatiously at works which only slowly material-ised. Thus the dissatisfaction increased to such an extent that it became the custom to stamp almost every diplomatic transaction as a "failure"

Dissatisfaction with the existing state of affairs engendered a desire for better things. The general public looked upon the predominance of the aristocracy and plutocracy in the service as the root of the evil, and demanded that more call should be made on *bourgeois* ability. Although here and there personal ambition may have been the driving force behind this demand, there can be no doubt that there was very great justification for it on the whole. The historical development of diplomacy, as well as the imperative requirements of not a few foreign posts, had in reality led to conditions which were no longer consistent with the spirit of the times. These difficulties had long been recognised in the responsible quarter, where a most honest wish to strike out new paths was felt, and had now and again been acted upon. Hard realities, for the most part beyond our control, stood in the way of its practical demonstration to any great extent, for a long time to come. What could be done, to begin with, in the direction of doing away with out of date conditions, was done. New and useful elements were introduced into the rising generation of the diplomatic service, and appointments were made on absolutely unexception-able principles. Instructions were given that the door was to be very widely opened to the diplomatic and consular professions, as far as name and origin were concerned, but strictly guarded, as regards knowledge and ability. Of course there were limits even to this. If all the suggestions made for the training of diplomats and consuls were to be adopted, the course would be so comprehensive, and, above all, so long, that there would hardly be any candidates willing to go through it. Moreover, knowledge is not sufficient, even when phenomenal. What a foreign representative needs, in addition to general education, is, above all, common-sense, clear insight, and tact.

If, in spite of the reorganisation of the diplomatic service which was resolutely taken in hand, with full knowledge of the requirements—I am speaking of the period before the war—complaints of shortcomings were still made, if people still talked of the inefficiency of German diplomacy, and a strong tendency was apparent, during and after the war, to hold the foreign representatives mainly responsible for the disastrous course of events, this can only be accounted for by the fact that want of knowledge of the circumstances led to the root of the evil being sought in the wrong quarter. This ignorance was in reality, and still is, lamentably great. Absolutely erroneous ideas still prevail in the widest circles as to the peculiar nature of diplomatic activity, as to its possibilities and impossibilities, as to the limits within which it is confined by existing custom, by the fixed rules of international law, and by the force of circumstances. People are only too prone to credit diplomacy with an efficacy it does not and cannot possess, and its representatives with far more authority and power and a wider sphere of influence that they ever have had or ever would have, no matter who they might be, and to expect them to accomplish tasks which would be quite beyond them, even if they were the most accomplished of supermen.

The course of events in the lives of peoples is often too powerful to be controlled by diplomacy. It is determined by forces whose sources and paths are not always accessible to personal influence. The great march of the political, economic, and cultural development of nations in an upward or downward direction, the growth, continued existence, or decay of vital national forces, decrees of fate which have a powerful effect for good or evil, historically rooted national ideals, strong movements and currents, lofty emotions which stir the soul of a nation, and waves of passion, these are things against whose elementary power the strongest and wisest diplomat is almost helpless with the resources at his disposal. These resources are, as a rule, limited to the spoken, written, and printed word. Skilful use of words may accomplish a good deal, on the other hand, even more may be ruined by their unskilful use. An accompaniment of jingling spurs and blows of the fist on the table, such as is not infrequently recommended by over-zealous German patriots, is out of place even towards smaller States, for these are the most sensitive. If it should so happen once in a way, that the application of stronger methods is under consideration, the decision as to this does not rest with the representative, but with the higher responsible quarter, on which the Ambassador is far more dependent than is generally understood. The days when an envoy was despatched with far-reaching powers and a free hand, bearing strife or understanding, war or peace, in the folds of his raiment, are over, now that there is wireless communication between one end of the world and the other. He takes no important step without the knowledge and wish of his Government, he has to carry out its instructions. As Bismarck said, " Ambassadors have to wheel about the same as non-commissioned officers."

This dependence on a central responsible quarter is imperative, for it is only there that all the information comes in which makes it possible to form a general idea of the position, and decide on the course to be taken. If a representative has serious objections to the instructions given by his Government, he can urge them, if there is time for this, which will very seldom be the case. If he does not approve of the general drift of the policy of his country, or if a particular step seems to him disastrous, and the objections he urges are unavailing, then—he can go. If it were really a question of a disaster, of course he would not avert it by doing so. If, as is evident from this, the representative's freedom of action is restricted, his sphere of action is no less strictly limited It only extends to the country in which he acts, he only holds to some extent in his own hands such scraps of the threads of high policy as connect it with this sphere. Within it, his busi-

ness is above all to observe, to form useful
connections in order to see below the surface,
to fathom the psychology of the national life,
to find means of exerting useful influence, and
finally to give his Government a detailed and
convincing report of the result of his observa-
tions. To draw conclusions and reach decisions
is again a matter for the central directorate of
foreign policy in his own country.

But even this quarter is by no means always
free as regards its decisions. Those responsible
will indeed be careful, like the General, not to
leave it to the enemy to decide on the line of
action, but it is not always their will which
creates the position to be mastered The history
of peace as well as of war, particularly of the
world-war, abounds in instances of forces other
than those of diplomacy, competent or otherwise, interfering in the course of events in such
a way as to force the political leaders into paths
they would never have taken had they acted on
their own unfettered judgment.

There is one thing more to be considered :
diplomacy not infrequently inherits embarrassing
and unenviable legacies, and has to accept responsibility for circumstances which it has had
no share in bringing about. There are also
situations and isolated events which lead to difficulties with other nations, for which no one in
a responsible position on either side is to blame.
Incidents, misunderstandings, different views of
the law, and similar things which fall, as it
were, like bolts from the blue. Finally, it must
be remembered that the work of diplomacy is

not only influenced by counter-work on the enemy side, but also by counter-work at home. Not only has diplomacy " to mend the windows the stones thrown by the Press have broken," but it sometimes has to repair even worse damage. It has only too frequently happened that its tedious Penelope work has been undone, or suddenly torn to pieces, by clumsy hands.

Although it may seem from these statements that there was very little justification for the poor opinion held in Germany of German diplomacy, it must be admitted that, like every other human institution, the diplomatic service was neither perfect nor infallible. Mistakes were made, both great and small, both by higher officials and subordinates, but they were isolated, and were compensated for by a vast amount of good and successful work. Far more useful work might have been done in many ways had we had the same amount of weapons at our disposal as other States. Those whose opinions had matured under pressure of the years of war, and of its experiences, were right in this respect in pointing to the insufficient use of propaganda. The inadequacy, however, was not so much in its use, as in the extent of the funds available for the purpose. Here again was a shortcoming which had been recognised in good time, and painfully felt in the responsible quarter, but the help needed to remedy it was not forthcoming

As Secretary of State I submitted a scheme in 1910 for more extensive Press activity, which was favourably received by the Federal Council and the Reichstag. But, in the long run, the demand for considerably increased funds was rejected by the Majority of the Reichstag. The scheme was frustrated by the opposition, on principle, of the Liberals on the one hand, and mainly, on the other, by the opposition of the section of the Centrum Party influenced by Erzberger. There was a suspicion in this quarter that the funds might be diverted to domestic political purposes, to fighting the Centrum Party, instead of being exclusively applied to the purposes for which they were voted. I was told in confidence that this distrust did not in any way apply to me personally; I could count on liberal credits if I would do justice to the existing feeling by making certain personal changes in the Press Section without delay. It was all the less possible for me to yield to this unreasonable demand as, in doing so, I should have been acting in opposition to the Chancellor's views and wishes.

I confess that my experience of how the strength of foreign policy can be crippled by the narrow party standpoint, and by unreasonable prejudice, had no little influence on my decision to resign.

Not only was there much talk at that time of striking out new paths in selecting and training foreign representatives, but also of the necessity for a change in the spirit and organisation of the Foreign Office. There was justification for these demands too, although they were for the most part based on the mistaken view, encouraged by the *Daily Telegraph* affair, that the Office had become a centre of hidebound bureaucracy. The spirit prevailing among these officials was really less prejudiced, and far more adapted to modern requirements than was commonly believed. The capacity for work and the rapid but scrupulously thorough execution of the many-sided and ever-increasing tasks, left nothing to be desired The old machinery of the ceaseless business worked, apart from the *Daily Telegraph* incident, without a hitch. But it was so out of date that it had to be replaced by something new and better, that was a necessity which was nowhere earlier recognised than in the office itself. Attempts were repeatedly made to reorganise it thoroughly, but they came to nothing, owing to the difficulties which were particularly great at the time of the great financial reform. We had to manage as best we could with trifling remedies and alleviations of the technical difficulties. More important changes had to be postponed till a more favourable moment.

The introduction of the regional system was contemplated even at that time. Lack of cohesion was remedied, as far as possible, by conferences between directors, and individual absolutely necessary intermediary and connecting links were formed. In addition to the financial difficulties, there was another great obstacle in the way of further progress in the desired direction, namely, the burden it imposed on the Secretary of State. He could not devote his whole energy to so difficult a task as investigating and carrying out thorough reform, unless the heavy load of work attached to his position were lightened. There were obstacles in the way of this which must not be underrated. I did not feel I could entrust the great work of reform to other hands consistently with my responsibility. There were indeed plenty of capable hands, but in view of the shortage in the higher personnel, they were not free—a *circulus vitiosus.*

The question of a new constitution for Alsace-Lorraine, which was discussed in 1910, pertained to the sphere of domestic Imperial policy. But it was one of those questions whose solution may influence foreign policy I was therefore requested to attend the meeting of the Prussian Ministry at which the attitude to be adopted in the Federal Council towards this question was to be considered. In answer to the question whether restricted or liberal consideration of the wishes of the inhabitants would be advisable from the standpoint of foreign policy, I said that concession of the autonomy to which they aspired appeared to me best. It would not only satisfy the people of Alsace-Lorraine, but would pacify France to a certain extent, and thus help to relieve the tension between us and France. If Alsace-Lorraine were placed on the same footing as the other States forming the Empire, such a manifestation of proud confidence in the solidity of the extended foundation walls of the Imperial structure, could not but have a very sobering effect on the French, who were wont to speak of the existing state of affairs as only provisional. Not a few Frenchmen, all of whom are sensitive as regards their honour, would look on the concession of such an important position to the former French provinces as somewhat of an atonement, and a first step in the direction of better relations between the two countries. Such a solution might release forces on the French side which had not been strong enough to come to the surface hitherto. The fear that it would strengthen French influence in Alsace-Lorraine did not seem to me well-founded. The sound common-sense of the overwhelmingly German population would be a stronger barrier in the way of undesirable French penetration than bureaucratic supervision.

Unfortunately I was alone in this view, even the Chancellor did not share it, and as I was neither a member of the Cabinet, nor had I a vote in it, my expression of opinion had no effect. Later events showed that my suggestion was worthy of a better fate than to have been ignored. Herr von Bethmann-Hollweg has frankly admitted in his *Betrachtungen zum Weltkrieg* that it was a mistake not to have conceded autonomy. An effort was made to remedy this mistake towards the end of the war, but it was too late !

The question of a constitution for the Imperial provinces was not, however, the only instance of those responsible for the management of foreign affairs being confronted with difficulties, in consequence of due importance not being attached to their opinion, if indeed it was asked at all. ' Thus it is well known that canal construction was decided on in Prussia, which must have the effect of considerably raising the shipping dues. Not only the States which were parties to the Elbe and Rhine treaties, Holland and Austria, but also some of the Federal States individually strongly opposed the scheme as they were annoyed at no attempt having been made to reach an understanding in good time. The equally thankless and hopeless task of subsequently trying to overcome these difficulties then devolved upon the Foreign Office.

' It was the same in the case of the Danish policy pursued by the Prussian home authorities, which was not only an obstacle in the way of amicable relations with Denmark, but was also responsible for the breakdown of a commercial treaty which had been negotiated with this economically important neighbouring country. The Foreign Office fully recognised that the failure of efforts to turn the Danish - speaking population of our Northern Mark into good' Germans, gave our home authorities a good deal of annoyance and justified corresponding measures being taken, but it was of opinion that an importance, which might prejudice the relations between the two countries, ought not to be attached to grievances which were really very trifling in numerical proportion to the population of the Empire. Disagreements arose even with our Austro-Hungarian ally, in consequence of the harsh Prussian policy in the East Mark and the practice of expulsion, against which the Foreign Office had frequently had occasion to protest without any practical result. This may have been due to the more or less plainly evident feeling that too much consideration was being shown for foreign countries.

Court duties were no small addition to the burden of current official business. They made far more claim on the time of the Secretary

of State for Foreign Affairs than on that of other
Ministers, as he had to attend not only the
great State entertainments, but every function in
connection with foreign visits and those from
the Federal States, as well as in connection with
members of the diplomatic corps, special Missions,
Congresses, etc. Functions of this kind were
sometimes so numerous that they succeeded one
another without a pause. Although now and again
this gave an opportunity of coming into useful
contact with important personages, the political
importance of the meetings was too trifling, in
most cases, to compensate for the loss of time.
Only a few of them were worth mentioning as
having affected policy. A visit from the Archduke
Franz Ferdinand, with his wife, led to a slight
conflict between political considerations and Court
usages. Policy spoke in favour of the Archduke's morganatic wife, as well as the Archduke
himself, being received with every mark of distinction, Court etiquette against it. There were
consequently differences of opinion which even
led to the Empress calling on the Imperial
Chancellor and trying to induce him to abandon
the political considerations. But Herr von Beth-
mamm-Hollweg was firm, and the visit went off with
the desired smoothness.

One or two curious and rather amusing things
happened on other occasions. Two Chinese
Missions, which had been sent to study our
naval and military system, were received with
great ceremony. When the second of these
Missions was waiting for the Kaiser in the
Muschelsaal of the New Palace, a difficulty

arose owing to the Kaiser, who was suffering from a boil on the arm, being unable to get into the sleeve of his uniform, on account of the thick bandage. The Kaiser's old valet so strongly opposed the suggestion that a slit should be made in the seam of the sleeve, that the attempt had to be abandoned. Fortunately the Crown Prince came so quickly, in response to a telephonic message, that he was able to hold the reception for the Kaiser without any great delay.

A visit from the former President of the United States, Mr. Theodore Roosevelt, also took rather an unexpected turn. He was visiting European capitals, for the purpose of giving lectures, on his way back from a shooting expedition in the Egyptian Sudan, and although he now only ranked as a private individual, the Kaiser, in his zeal to make friendly advances to distinguished Americans, intended that Mr. Roosevelt and his family should stay at the Castle in Berlin. I knew from Mr. Hill that Mr. Roosevelt would gladly have escaped such an unusual mark of distinction. It would not have been properly understood in America either, and I was just going to let the Kaiser know this, when the news of King Edward's death arrived. The Court mourning necessitated the reception being of a simple nature. Here, again, an unlucky star seemed to be in the ascendant. It had been announced that the train from Copenhagen in which Mr. Roosevelt was coming, would be very late. Consequently, when it arrived, having almost overtaken the time lost, there was no one at the station to receive him officially. This visit, however, went off without any further *contre-temps*. The Kaiser was delighted with the former President's blunt manliness, and overwhelmed him with kindness. It is well known, from the hostile atttitude Mr. Roosevelt ostentatiously adopted towards Germany during the war, how little permanent effect this had.

Although I had successfully withstood the many attacks made on me by my opponents, a memory remained of the way in which the conflict had been carried on which made me feel it better not to enter the arena again. I also doubted whether I could give the Chancellor the assistance he needed. We were too much alike at heart to form a whole which could guarantee a conduct of foreign policy in conformity with the national sentiment. Both of us were more inclined to weigh carefully, and act cautiously, than to take rapid decisions and give a strong lead. To all this was added impaired health, which made a period of rest, or at all events a less exhausting occupation, seem imperative. Consequently, in the summer of 1910, I decided to resign the Secretaryship of State for Foreign Affairs, and accept the post of Ambassador in Paris, which had been offered me. I had not applied for this appointment ; the Chancellor had, on the contrary, offered me the choice between resuming office after an interval of sick leave, or taking over the Paris post, in which it was found necessary to make a change, the then Ambassador being no longer equal to the requirements.

My belief was that Herr von Kiderlen was the man of all others to succeed me at the Foreign Office, as he had the qualifications which seemed requisite under the existing conditions. Herr von Bethmann-Hollweg had also thought of him, but there was a doubt as to whether the choice might not be opposed by the Kaiser, who had a disagreeable recollection of the time when Kiderlen had accompanied him on his travels, and had sometimes indulged too freely in his natural love of a joke. The Kaiser, however, subordinated his personal feelings to political considerations, and sanctioned the proposed personal change. It was remarked at that time that my resignation was not accompanied by a written communication from the Cabinet, and this gave rise to a rumour that there was something wrong as far as I was concerned. The truth is that such communications were not customary in the case of Secretaries of State holding Imperial offices, as the competence of the Prussian Civil Cabinet did not extend to them. I had, however, received a friendly message of farewell from the Kaiser, but had not published it. It was a telegram from Kiel, as follows :—

I rely on your serving me as well and faithfully' in Paris as in the post you have held hitherto. I am having my signed photograph forwarded to you in remembrance of the Berlin days. Gratefully,

(*Signed*) WILLIAM I R.

The official position I held to a certain extent necessarily involved my seeing a good deal of the Kaiser personally. In accordance with tradition and his own inclination he took great interest in foreign policy, and wished to be kept *au courant* of all that went on, and approached for his approval or decision in matters of importance. This led to my being in constant official communication with him either in writing or by word of mouth. In addition to this, Court functions frequently brought me in contact with him. The Kaiser facilitated the daily official intercourse considerably by dispensing with the troublesome formalities of Court etiquette which are otherwise customary. When he was in Berlin he was in the habit of calling on the Chancellor or me, or on both of us, early in the morning, and dealing with the matters under consideration as he strolled about the beautiful gardens. Although the Kaiser was in the habit of putting his own opinion and wishes first, he was not at all inaccessible to objections or adverse opinions ; he was, on the contrary, always ready to give due weight to his responsible adviser's suggestions, and generally approved of them. He expected absolute candour, and there were consequently repeated occasions on which it seemed advisable to tell him things which could not have been very pleasant, or to endeavour to secure decisions which he could not have found it easy to take

Never did the Kaiser protest against these efforts, or show the smallest sign of annoyance As far as his decisions with regard to personal questions are concerned, there is no justification for the legend current in Germany that he generally followed his own inclinations. I know of no instance in which the Kaiser did not agree to the proposal made by the responsible head as to filling higher posts, nor do I know of a single instance in which the question of an Ambassador or Minister's private means was even passingly alluded to. If, in spite of this constant intercourse, and in spite of the Kaiser's earnest wish not to deal with foreign policy without responsible guidance, he sometimes said and did things which went beyond the prescribed limits, this can be accounted for by a temperament, tempestuous in his youth, and still extraordinarily excitable in his riper years, which could not resist the impulses of the moment, the temptation of a supposed harmless opportunity, and the intense craving to assert himself.

The Kaiser's was quite an unusual personality; in many ways highly gifted, in other ways childishly simple, he was more open-hearted and ingenuous than a man of calm superior judgment. Inspired by an earnest desire to administer his exalted office faithfully, in accordance with the laws of God and man, full of ambitious ideas and confidence that he would be given strength to carry them out. Endowed with a receptive mind, power of quick comprehension, an astonishing memory, a facility in speaking and writing which was a temptation to him, thoroughly well-informed in some and only superficially so in other branches of knowledge, free from old-fashioned prejudices, and yet a believer in the grace of God, frequently too peremptory, then again feeling his way and hesitating, generally convinced that what he did was right, sometimes torn with doubts and self-condemnation. His restless eager activity repeatedly came to a standstill, unknown to the general public; he was seized with fits of despondency, and had thoughts of abdicating. At such times of mental depression, it needed all the Empress's powers of persuasion to revive his courage and induce him to carry on his office, promising to 'do better.

One of the Kaiser's weakest points was his lack of insight into human character, a result of the narrowness of Court life. Trusting others over much, he looked for equal confidence in return, and expected to receive it from individual personal friends. In this he was profoundly disappointed, but he took it too deeply to heart to feel any bitterness. He was for the most part denied the gifts which would have been of most use to him as a ruler, such as a capacity for cool, careful, and prudent reflection. A one-sided education, his having been called early to the throne, and the flattery and ever-increasing admiration of the age he lived in, did not conduce to fill the gaps in the lesson of life. Taken all round, a man with great merits but considerable shortcomings, not a well-balanced mind. In public life the imperious pompous ruler, in the quiet of his home life a human being like others, a good man, whose simplicity and refreshing candour were very attractive. It would be difficult to decide which was most consistent with the Kaiser's true character, his simple manner in private life or his sensational attitude in public. It is a psychological question which only the few can ask to whom both were familiar. Whatever the verdict may tend to be, the judges will retain more memory of the bright than of the dark side of the picture, thanks to nature's kindly gift of implanting pleasant more firmly than unpleasant recollections in our minds.

IV

AMBASSADOR IN PARIS

I WAS appointed Ambassador in Paris during one of those periods of calm which are apt to succeed periods of anxiety. The settlement of the Casablanca incident, and the Morocco agreement of February 1909, had not been without a beneficial influence on the strained feeling on both sides. The phrase " friendly and neighbourly relations " was used for the first time in the course of the conversations which took place, according to custom, on the occasion of my formal reception by President Fallières. I had not selected the expression as it were at random. It expressed a wish sincerely felt in responsible quarters in Berlin, where it had been carefully considered. But although the feeling may consequently have seemed favourable to a better understanding, there could be no doubt that our relations to our western neighbour were now as ever influenced by the great question of Alsace-Lorraine. In spite of forty years having elapsed since the events which had led to France being seriously defeated, and suffering painful loss both of territory, power, and prestige, in spite of the country having achieved renewed prosperity and settled down to peace after pro-

longed domestic struggles, of its having increased
its strength by the acquisition of extensive and
valuable colonial possessions, and long since recovered the position of a great Power, as the
result of a wise policy, the wound of 1871
would not heal, the French still demanded
satisfaction for the injury to their national
pride.

Time had not indeed been without effect, the
clamour for restoration of "the lost provinces"
was less persistent and menacing than in the
days of the *revanche*, General Boulanger and the
patriot Déroulède, but recovery of what had been
lost was still the ideal to which the soul of the
nation clung. This aim was the pivot on which
French policy turned throughout. Even the periods
of calm made no difference as to this. Satisfactory as they might be in themselves, they
could not be looked upon as an indication that
the aim had been abandoned, or as anything
more than halting-places on the road to its attainment, postponement of decisive action. The position
was never at any time such that a Government in France could have continued in office
which took any step seeming to imply recognition of the Frankfurt treaty of peace, even at
times when public opinion had calmed down.
The majority of the people were naturally less
fired with patriotic excitement as time went on,
but an active minority, with effective means at
its disposal, was unremitting in its efforts to
keep up the smouldering fire, with a view to
its bursting into flames at the given moment.
And in no country has the theory that active

minorities are able to carry the more passive majority with them been more clearly demonstrated than in France. There were times when France's attention was diverted, under the guidance of far-seeing statesmen, from the " gap in the Vosges " to seeking an outlet for her national energies in great colonial undertakings, and when she gained a great deal in that direction, but a clever and pushing group invariably succeeded in bringing about a swing of the pendulum by seizing the moment when some failure had given dissatisfaction, and once more convincing the soul of the people that the old aim, Alsace-Lorraine, was the one to which all their energies should be turned.

France's general policy was unmistakably dominated by hostility to Germany, with the exception of occasional agreement in individual questions which were totally independent of the great point of disagreement. Everything done in the way of high policy was only with the one object, the creation of better prior conditions for a future reckoning with Germany. This led, first of all, to the alliance with Russia and the special military agreements which followed, and, ten years later, to the *entente cordiale,* the friendship with England France was eager to cement more and more closely, and which involved an almost humiliating effort to overcome the old bitter enmity.

When this important success had been achieved, another period of comparative peace set in. This was to be accounted for by the satisfactory consciousness of having found compensation for the weakness resulting from the steady decrease in the birth-rate, in the human material and other sources of help from the colonies, as well as in the support of powerful allies and friends, and of being thus armed to fight Germany, when the time came, with every prospect of success.

Under these circumstances, the course for me to pursue in Paris was clear. It was obvious that the inability of the French nation to accommodate itself to the existing position was the real source of European unrest, the cause of all the trouble, and of the necessity for excessive expenditure on armaments. Although it would have been hopeless to think of beginning by trying to do away with this fountain head of trouble, it was within the bounds of possibility to diminish its underlying tributaries on the one hand, and on the other to divert its overflow into a direction in which it might gradually exhaust itself. At all events, it seemed worth while to make cautious efforts in that sense. Of course, it was essential that they should as little consist in making ostentatious advances, which had been done here and there without permanent success, as in adopting an overbearing attitude which would offend the easily wounded French susceptibilities. If we wished the seeds of a better understanding to germinate, it was essential that we should carefully consider the steps to be taken, having regard to their effect on the political sensibility of the French people. A quiet, dignified, but chivalrously courteous attitude on the whole, with here and there an understanding in matters quite outside the danger zone, seemed alone likely to create an atmosphere which would produce and encourage the growth of a better feeling.

Careful observation soon confirmed my view that, without abandoning its ideals, the French nation was peaceably disposed on the whole, and not inclined to be driven into risky adventures by nationalistic agitators. It seemed likely that the progress made in the process of pacification would be all the steadier the more we avoided throwing any obstacle in the way of it, and above all took care not to do anything which could excite the ultra-sensitive patriotic feeling of the French, and bring grist to the mill of the *revanche* preachers.

The early days of my activity in Paris opened up a fairly hopeful prospect of things taking the desired course. Schemes were drawn up for working hand in hand in the spirit of the Morocco agreement, not only in the Shereefian Empire, but also in more distant African regions. Various undertakings of this kind, mostly suggested by Germany, very nearly materialised. They were not made the subject of official negotiations, and were only confidentially discussed in the first instance, but there was just as much readiness to further them in French as in German official quarters. Many French statesmen made strenuous efforts to secure their success, but this very fact, which seemed so satisfactory, proved a disadvantage in the long run ; it led to friction between the politicians who were striving for the upper hand, and to confusion in which the plans were swallowed up one after another.

Even Morocco was soon to prove once more

a Pandora box.   Some of France's military and
political representatives there found it difficult to
reconcile the situation created by treaties and agreements with their ambitions, and could not resist
the temptation to overstep the limits drawn, in a
way which only thinly disguised the intention of
making further headway.   Risings took place in
Tunis, which afforded a welcome opportunity for
interposing, and finally led to a military expedition
against the Sultan's towns of Fez and Mekinez, for
the purpose of rescuing the Europeans, who were
alleged to be in danger in these places in the
interior of the country, and, after insignificant
fighting, to their occupation.   We knew what
value to attach to the assurance given by the
French Government that this occupation was only
to be temporary, and would cease as soon as order
was restored, from previous French examples in
North Africa, and from the English precedent
in Egypt, when equally emphatic assurances were
given

We did not fail to warn the French against
advancing in Morocco in contravention of the
treaty   The matter was represented to the French
Ambassador in Berlin by the Imperial Chancellor, and by me to the Ministers in Paris.
Things seemed to be getting beyond the French
Government, however—the Premier, M. Monis, and
the Minister for Foreign Affairs, M. Cruppi—
it was not strong enough to resist the military
pressure, and to estimate the story that Europeans
were in danger of their lives in the Sultan's territory
at its true value.   It was fully realised in Paris
that the action taken went far beyond the limits

of justifiable police intervention, and was consequently not in accordance with the treaties and agreements ; it was also impossible to suppose that in our anxiety to avoid friction we should remain passive spectators of doings which must very considerably prejudice our treaty rights and interests. The French conscience was not altogether easy, and it was assumed that nothing but compensation for our losses would secure our consent to the change in the' position in Morocco. But the Government could not make up its mind to take steps which might have given reason to believe that France was willing to adjust the matter in this way, although we left time for such a decision to be reached. Hence the German Government felt obliged to protest, and in order to expedite matters the gunboat *Panther* was sent to the southern Atlantic coast of Morocco.

I had nothing to do with the decision to take this step, nor had I been informed of the plan in such a way as to give me an opportunity of expressing an opinion. I had, indeed, heard incidentally that a demonstration was contemplated, but I did not know what its nature or extent would be, or where and when it would take place, until I received instructions to inform the French Government that the ship had been despatched, and to represent that our economic interests in the south of Morocco, the Sûs district, were endangered by impending risings, apparently provoked by what had occurred in other parts of the country, and that we therefore felt obliged to afford help and shelter to the Germans and others under our protection in those districts, in case of need. As soon as peace and order were restored in Morocco, the ship would leave Agadir. This was a hint not to be misunderstood, and a plain assertion of our rights.

In spite of the French conscience not being clear, and of the fact that warning voices had been raised, notably that of M. Jaurès, the news of the step we had taken fell like a bombshell in Paris. Its first effect was to produce consternation and perplexity. This was increased by the fact that a new Government had just come into power under the former Minister of Finance, M. Caillaux, with M. de Selves, a new importation, as Foreign Minister, a Government which was credited with the intention of bringing about better relations with Germany. Had these good intentions been apparent earlier, there might probably have been a question of our waiting a little longer before taking action in the first instance, but the change of Government had been effected with the startling rapidity which is not uncommon in France, and under circumstances to which the current saying that " a bit of orange peel " sometimes brings about the fall of Ministries, was very applicable.

As things were, we had shot our arrow, and everything depended on whether the French Government would make up its mind to take steps which had hitherto been omitted, in the direction of an agreement with us. It would not be easy, for public opinion was roused to a furious pitch over our procedure, which was regarded as a coercive measure   The difficulties of the position were increased by, the fact that the Foreign Minister was just going to accompany M. Fallières on a visit of several days to the Dutch ·Court. Nevertheless, although I did not succeed in getting a definite answer from him before he left, he went so far as to say : " *Je ne dis pas non.*" M. Caillaux himself took over the duties of the Foreign Office during the few days, and in view of his personal way of thinking, this gave some hope that the Government would not evade a discussion with us   But even M   Caillaux still hesitated. He turned to the English friend for advice, and seems to have received an answer to the effect that it would be advisable to take the wind out of the interloper's sails by a counterattack, and oblige him to withdraw.   M. Caillaux, however, did not quite like the idea of this ; he wanted first to see whether the matter would end with our mere demonstration at Agadir, or whether we should land troops and gain a footing in the country   This hesitation was not at all in accordance with the views of the English Government, which had deliberately credited us, without further ado, with the intention of getting a footing on the Atlantic coast of Morocco, and now thought it necessary to fortify the wavering French friend.   The method chosen was Mr. Lloyd George's well-known speech, in which he tried to intimidate us by using threatening language.   The very proper exception we took to this presumption had a sobering effect on the French too, and when the Foreign Minister returned from Holland, I found his frame of mind so much improved that he was evidently willing to discuss the matter.

M. de Selves would have liked the negotiations to be carried on in Paris, a demand on which I threw cold water at once, as not being suitable under the circumstances. In my opinion, it was essential that it should be made perfectly clear to the outside world as well, that it was not for us but for France to make advances, and coming to Berlin would be the proper way of doing this. On the other hand I helped to set the negotiations on foot to the extent of having hinted to the Minister, in reply to his enquiry, that as far as I knew, an offer from France of part of the Congo as compensation for any injury to our interests in Morocco would be well received in Berlin. On this, the French Ambassador, Jules Cambon, who was staying in Paris, received instructions to return to Berlin and start the negotiations. The French Government had also applied to its Russian allies for advice, but found they did not take more than a lukewarm interest in the matter. On the other hand, M. Isvolsky, who was now the Russian Ambassador in Paris, was unremitting in his efforts to work on the French susceptibilities. It was out of the question, he said, to enter into negotiations with any one who placed "a loaded revolver" on the table from the start.

Spain, who had a territorial *status* to safeguard in North Morocco, and had no little trouble in maintaining the relations established by treaty with France without friction, took more interest in the matter. She did not wish any one but herself to gain a footing in the south, opposite the Canary Islands. M. Perez Caballero, the Spanish Ambassador, who had so definitely taken part against us at Algeciras, now approached me with a request to be allowed to take part in the negotiations, of course with the intention of siding with us. I forwarded the suggestion to Berlin at once, recommending its adoption, but it did not meet with approval there. The course of events gave reason to regret this attitude later on. It obliged Spain to come to an understanding with France alone, not to our advantage, and she was all the more annoyed at her wishes being disregarded, as she was inclined to join the Triple Alliance, but a feeler she had thrown out in Vienna some time before had been coldly received.

The negotiations in Berlin only progressed slowly, owing to the difficulties of the questions at issue. France, indeed, was willing to fall in with our wish that a considerable share of her Congo territory should be made over to us, but it was not easy to find natural boundaries which would satisfy the wishes and requirements of both parties The French Government, and particularly M. Caillaux personally, tried to reduce our demands in the Congo basin by offering compensation elsewhere. There was still a very wide difference between the two points of view, when Herr von Kiderlen, the Secretary of State for Foreign Affairs, who was much in need of a rest, took advantage of a pause in the negotiations to go off to Chamonix. I had some difficulty in appeasing the annoyance felt in Paris over what was considered an offensive want of tact. The truth was that

Herr von Kiderlen had inadvertently overlooked the fact that Chamonix was on French ground. None the less the incident left an impression which was not favourable to the further course of the negotiations. At the same time I succeeded in obtaining agreement in principle to a solution which would have secured us wide access to the Congo basin, not only the two headlands to the Ubangi conceded later on. The proposal subsequently fell to the ground again in the further course of the negotiations.

The longer the solution of the whole disputed question was delayed, the more strongly influences in Paris prejudiced the *bonne volonté* which had not been altogether lacking at first on the part of the French Government. I repeatedly called the attention of the Berlin Government to this, and urged the negotiations being expedited as much as possible, lest Caillaux's Ministry should be defeated by the increasingly strong Opposition That it remained in power until after the treaty was concluded was due to the Opposition not wishing to imperil the treaty itself, which promised to give France the advantage of a freer hand in Morocco, or to incur responsibility for the serious consequences of the negotiations breaking down. But M. Caillaux's opponents, led by the old hand at overthrowing Ministries, Clemenceau, could not forgive him for having not only yielded to the pressure we exerted to bring about negotiations, but having taken advantage of the opportunity to propose further agreements, with a view to relieving the general tension, and what is more, having done this covertly, without reference to the responsible Minister for Foreign Affairs. Consequently, the Ministry was overthrown after the conclusion of the treaty, advantage being taken of a side issue which arose in the course of the debate in the Senate. The treaty itself was ratified.

M. Caillaux's Government was succeeded by a Ministry formed of the strongest available forces, under the leadership of M. Raymond Poincaré, who took over the Foreign Office as well. The change of Government had in itself meant a reversal of M Caillaux's conciliatory policy, but this was made even clearer by the speech announcing the new Government's programme, which laid special stress on dignity, strength, and self-respect, as well as careful cultivation of the alliance with Russia and the friendship with England, both of which M. Caillaux had been inclined to neglect. Consequently, a nationalistic Government and a programme which might be briefly summarised in the words : " France will not tolerate a second Agadir."

The treaty with regard to Morocco and the Congo, which was concluded on November 4, 1911, did not give satisfaction either on the German or the French side. The feeling which prevailed in Germany was one of disappointment at the trifling extent and doubtful value of the territorial gains in Central Africa, whereas injured *amour propre* was mainly responsible for the dissatisfaction felt in France. The French people found it difficult to reconcile themselves to having been ingloriously compelled, under pressure bordering on extortion, to give up colonial territory which owed its exploitation to the French spirit of enterprise, only gaining in return a free hand politically but not economically in Morocco, which their ambition had led them to look upon as a country exclusively reserved for French activity. The chief value of the treaty, the removal of a constant source of friction between us and France, was indeed secretly appreciated by many, but no one ventured to own to this in public. Far from improving the relations between us and France, the new agreement, unlike the one of 1909, produced somewhat of a state of irritation which was responsible for not a few difficulties in carrying it out, all the more as M. Poincaré himself was the personification of the new spirit of greater *amour propre* and more hopeless obstinacy. Efforts were continually made on the French side to interpret individual provisions of the treaty to our disadvantage, or to ignore our claims based on former agreements. And even when we succeeded in getting our rights and interests respected in Paris, by firmly insisting on them, it only too often happened that we could get no further than this, owing to the high-handed behaviour of the French officials in Morocco, who were all the more arbitrary, the more subordinate their positions.

The Italian expedition to Tripoli must be looked upon as a result of the French acquisition of Morocco, which began with the expedition to Fez. Granted that domestic political reasons may have prompted the Italian Government to pave the way for the nation to acquire a colonial sphere of influence on the other side of the Mediterranean, granted also that the idea of asserting a claim to a share in Mediterranean supremacy may not have been new, still there can be no doubt that the decision to embark on the enterprise was influenced by the French advance, an advance which was not confined to Morocco, but extended to the hinterland of the States on the north coast of Africa. M. Tittoni, the Italian Ambassador in Paris, formerly Minister for Foreign Affairs, and a man of great political influence in his own country, was of opinion that the moment to take possession of the last remaining territory under Turkish rule in North Africa must be turned to account, unless they wanted to be overshadowed by French Imperialism and to forfeit a future to which they had a right. The French were, in fact, suspiciously active in the Tripoli hinterland, and plenty of Frenchmen, whose voices carried weight, were proclaiming the theory that France must acquire the whole of North Africa, from the ocean to the country of the Nile.

Italy had partly secured the consent of the Powers to the step she proposed taking years before, and she partly secured it now, with more or less trouble. The unfortunate position in which it would place us, between our ally and our friendship with Turkey, did not give her any serious anxiety. The only thing that could temper the annoyance to us and to Austria-Hungary was the doubtful prospect of Italy's being able to strengthen her position in the Mediterranean, and thereby increase her value as an ally. The enterprise, as is well known, was not quite as successful as had been hoped ; the Italian forces encountered obstinate resistance, although they were considerable, and were unable to accomplish more than the conquest of the coast region. In addition to this there were unpleasantnesses with England, who took possession of the harbour of Solum, and slight friction with France, which all the fine talk about the friendship between the Latin sister nations did not help to remove. Italy had occasion to complain bitterly of the way in which munitions were being smuggled into the country from Tunis by the French, and was obliged to seize two French steamboats which were carrying contraband. This gave rise to heated discussions in interviews and Notes, and in the Press and Parliaments, which put Franco-Italian friendship to a severe test, so much so, indeed, that France thought it necessary to transfer the whole of her fleet to the Mediterranean, clearly as a demonstration against Italy. The Italian idea of attacking Turkey's European possessions, which obtained for a time, having met with justifiable opposition from Austria-Hungary, and an attempt to force the Dardanelles having failed, Italy proceeded to occupy twelve islands in the Ægean Sea—the Dodecanese—thereby cutting off Turkey from Tripoli, and this put an end to the Turkish resistance. The peace of Lausanne, by which Turkey recognised Italian supremacy in Libya, ended the war. There was no occasion for us to discuss it with France, and I was able to confine my rôle in Paris to that of an onlooker.

The Moroccan and Tripolitan meteorological disturbances had not been got over, when a fresh storm gathered in the Balkans, the European storm centre. The Balkan War broke out, bring-

ing in its train the Albanian question. Although
the mainspring of the trouble was to be found
in the antagonisms between the nationalities
and Turkish maladministration, which were increased rather than diminished by the reforms forced
on them by the Powers, led by Russia, and
clumsily taken in hand by the Young Turks,
still the outbreak of strife and its intensity seem
to have been a result of the severe blow the
Italian enterprise had given the Turkish Empire,
and in a secondary degree, of the French offensive
against the Mussulman world in North Africa.
The Balkan nations thought the time had come
for them to break up European Turkey for
their part, and divide the spoil. They united
under Russia's obliging leadership in forming
the Balkan League, and in giving a death-blow
to the rule from Constantinople in the Balkan
War. In view of the difference in the attitude
of the Great Powers, of whom the one honestly,
the others only ostensibly, upheld the principle
of maintaining Turkey's territorial integrity, as
well as the existing antagonism between Austria-
Hungary and Russia, both of whom aspired to
supremacy in the Balkans, wide circles were
involved in the complications. France was less
directly than indirectly concerned through the
alliance with Russia and her friendship with
England, just as we were indirectly interested
through our alliances with Austria-Hungary and
Italy. This, as well as the need on both sides
for a respite after an agitating time, produced
a certain similarity in our positions which might
be turned to good account. M. Poincaré was

not blind to this, and lent a willing ear to our suggestion that we should try to restrain the more closely concerned Powers accessible to our respective influence, so that, to our great satisfaction, we were associated with France for a time in efforts to avert serious friction between the Great Powers.

In view of the fact that, shortly before this, the Minister had paid a visit to St. Petersburg, that increased military preparations had then been agreed upon, on the lines that Russia was to expedite the construction of her strategical railway lines in our direction with French money, and France was to revive the three years' military service, that, in addition to this, Russia had been promised French support for the policy she had embarked upon, which aimed at Constantinople and had, above all, the destruction of Austria-Hungary in view, and that, even before the visit, a naval convention had been concluded which provided for France's Mediterranean fleet being stationed to the advantage of Russia, the activity promised towards relieving the tension would be all the more remarkable in proportion to its success and the perseverance shown.

Unfortunately, far from being a pacifying influence, French policy again more or less clearly followed in Russia's wake in the course of the crisis. What could only be concluded from outward signs at that time, has since been established by the Russian Ambassador Isvolsky's published reports. According to these, the French Premier told him from the beginning, when the storm-cloud gathered in the Balkans, that Russia could rely on the strongest diplomatic support from France, and on her military support, in case of conflict with Austria-Hungary and armed intervention on the part of Germany as a result of this A few weeks later he further stated that it was for Russia to take the initiative, and that in case of Russia's going to war, France would also go to war, as there was no doubt that Germany would come to Austria-Hungary,'s assistance. Experts were of opinion that the chances in a general war were very much' in favour of Russia and France. He had said the same thing to the Italian Ambassador. There was no mention of a reservation that the help would only be forthcoming in case of an unprovoked attack *on Russia* The statements consequently appear in the light of *carte blanche* to Russia to act at her own discretion, if not a direct encouragement to go to war.

M. Poincaré was also in active communication with England, with a view to securing joint military action on the part of the Triple Entente Powers The well-known agreements were reached as to military action in case of need, which were set forth in a correspondence between Sir Edward Grey and the French Ambassador, Paul Cambon. They were not in the form of an alliance, which both France and Russia would have liked. That would have been contrary to the principles of English policy. But they were agreements which could easily be given the character of an alliance at any time The French Government was not satisfied with these steps, however. On the contrary, at the time when Russia thought fit to

add weight to her voice in the Council of the
Powers by so-called test mobilisations in her
western districts, France also made military preparations, very quietly, it is true, but not so imper-
ceptibly as not to be evident to vigilant eyes.
And the French War Office was busily engaged
in working out the great schemes, in conjunction
with the Admiralty, which made the prospect of
war, as Isvolsky said, " appear opportune."

That, in spite of all this, the Balkan Pandora
box was finally shut down, after a fashion, at
the Ambassadors' Conference in London, was
certainly not thanks to French policy. It had,
indeed, been such that it alarmed even the Russian
ally, and prompted Count Benckendorff, the
Russian Ambassador in London, to write to his
Government that of all the Powers France was
the only one which, if it could not be said that
she wished for war, at least would envisage it
without regret. At any rate, France did not
work for a compromise; a compromise would
have meant peace, the alternative was war. The
Ambassadors' Conference was, indeed, able to
preserve peace between the Great Powers, thanks
to English and German mediation, but what remained was a fragile peace, more a latent state
of war, in which two groups of Powers, the
Triple Alliance and the Triple Entente, faced
one another in an atmosphere full of distrust
and tension.

In view of these circumstances, which were
only fully revealed later on, but whose effects
were for the most part perceptible at once, the
election of M. Poincaré to succeed M. Fallières

as President of the French Republic, at the beginning of 1913, could not be regarded as a step in the direction of easing the general situation. His victory was not achieved without difficulty, for the election was preceded by violent struggles, more behind the scenes than in public, between the Radicals and Socialists, the advocates of a pacific foreign policy, and the Right Republicans and Conservatives, who favoured a strong attitude. It was only as a result of a second ballot that he was elected by 429 against 327 votes. He owed his final success to the Nationalistic Right, whose support he had managed to gain by promising to postpone social reforms and revive the practice of sending a representative to the Vatican, consequently a modification of the policy of antagonism to the Church

Little more than a year earlier the majority of the people had welcomed the formation of Poincaré's Cabinet because French *amour propre* looked on it as a protest against the Agadir affront, and since then public opinion had supported the Government policy, in so far as it had been clear, in the belief that, without having adventures in view, it seemed to be strengthening France's position by deepening the alliance and friendship in a way which guaranteed the maintenance of peace. It had also been supported, because it made a stand against alleged presumptuous and high-handed German aims of expansion, and set its face against the German spirit of enterprise and German ability, whose penetration was becoming more and more inconvenient, but at the same time there were many sensible people who felt misgivings as to the new drift. Those who knew more of what was going on, and were able to see farther into the future than the multitude, showed signs of serious anxiety before the President's election, expressed in the brief whispered remark : " *Lui, Président, ce sera la guerre.*" Nevertheless, President Poincaré had carried the day, and there was still a hope that the new President's policy, tempered by the neutrality this position demanded, would be more pacific than when he was Prime Minister, but this was a feeble hope, and was soon extinguished.

The first speech the President addressed to the Chamber and the Senate was in the same spirit as his former utterances. " France," he said in his message, " must be great and strong, in the interests of civilisation and of peace. What we need above all is energy." His first public acts showed that he himself meant to set a good example in materialising this spirit of energy. He broke with the tradition which imposes great reserve on the President of the Republic, paid visits, accepted an immense number of invitations, and lost no opportunity of showing himself to the Parisians, of displaying his brilliant gift of oratory and being fêted and acclaimed. His behaviour was more that of a monarch than the quiet life of a President, and did not fail to have the expected effect on the populace. Thus he rapidly gained what he aspired to above all, popularity; his admirers increased in number from day to day, they looked on him as the leader of the nation, who would

11

manage to uphold its dignity under all circumstances, as the statesman who would succeed
in securing France an important and honoured
position among the Powers, most likely even
among the Great Powers, and understand how
to retrieve her losses, in addition to restoring
her high prestige. Although he himself was
cautious in what he said in public, and laid
stress on the word " peace," always, however,
with the significant addition, " but a peace with
honour," he was not averse, as a native of
Lorraine, to being honoured as such, and lauded
as the future vindicator of hopes which had never
died out, although at times they were not mentioned.

The President called on me in person soon
after he took over the duties of his office. On
this occasion, too, he made a special point of
his love of peace. He was a man of peace,
and it was to the knowledge of this that he
chiefly owed his election, and its favourable reception by the French people, who were absolutely
pacifically disposed. He also spoke calmly of
the armaments on both sides. It was regrettable
that all the continental Powers thought it necessary
to make such immense efforts in this direction, but
there was no doubt that each of the individual nations had good reason for their action ; he
was far from seeing a threat to France in the new
German Army Bill, and hoped we took a similar
view with regard to France He also spoke of
M. Delcassé's recent appointment to be Ambassador
in St. Petersburg. It would be a mistake if
people in Germany were to look on this as an
unfriendly act, as seemed to be the case ; there

was no occasion for this. He had first thought of the distinguished former Premier, M. Ribot, for the post, but he could not make up his mind to accept it. As the St. Petersburg post must be filled by a man of importance, the idea had occurred to him of offering it to Delcassé, who had just left the Ministry of Marine. Finally, the President again touched on the pacific disposition of the French people, and added that they would not indeed put up quietly with a "second Agadir." The latter remark was particularly significant. It not only accurately described the predominant feeling of the French nation, but the keynote of the Premier's policy hitherto and of his future policy as President of the Republic.

The President's first political action was the appointment of a new Cabinet which would carry out his policy, and whose most important task was to be the bold step of reintroducing the three years' military service, given up a few years before This required statesmen of great, almost merciless energy. The President found them in M. Barthou, who became Prime Minister, and M. Millerand, who took over the Ministry of War. Foreign Affairs were entrusted to M. Jonnard, the former Governor-General of Algiers, a man of quiet and courteous demeanour, to whom the post may probably have been given chiefly that he might pacify other countries, in the turmoil of the struggle there was certain to be over the three years' service. Simultaneously, the Ambassador Louis was recalled from St. Petersburg, and was replaced by the late Minister of Marine, M. Delcassé, formerly a well-known enemy of Germany, but who had been very guarded of late years, and had even occasionally denied his hostility to Germany. This appointment was officially represented as a mark of esteem due to the much-abused man, but it was easy to read between the lines of the Nationalistic Press that Delcassé's mission was to deepen the Russian alliance. That was, in fact, the intention. M. Delcassé's business was to induce the Russian Government to make ever greater preparations for war, and especially to urge measures being taken which would expedite mobilisation and the march westwards. He carried out this task during his short stay in St. Petersburg to the point when the rest could be left in the hands of purely military quarters. The well-known article in the St. Petersburg financial newspaper, from the pen of the Russian War Minister, which stated that the Russian army was strong and confident of victory, and that Russia was quite ready, may be considered some acknowledgment of his activity.

A further important step taken by the President was a visit to the English Court. This was significant as regards the direction in which he thought it advisable to start his efforts to secure support. Among the initiated it was said that his heart was set on obtaining a promise in London of an early return visit to Paris, as this would make a great impression on public opinion in both countries, and show the world how strong France was, and in what esteem she was held. M. Poincaré was not in so great a hurry to visit the ally in St. Petersburg, for in this case personal effort was hardly needed to cement the relationship more closely. This visit only took place more than a year later, after the English return visit, and shortly before the outbreak of war.

The armament fever which attacked the Continental Powers after the Balkan War was a severe strain on the general situation, and particularly on Franco-German relations. The fever rose to such a height in France that, heavily burdened as the nation already was in the matter of military expenditure, it accepted the further heavy burden of a return to three years' military service, partly of its own accord, but mainly at Russia's instigation, and without even the former mitigations and exemptions. The French people visited their wrath on us, accused us of having given the signal for such inordinate and dangerous over-exertions, and hated us accordingly Although it was obvious to every impartial observer that the change in the general position, as a result of the Balkan War, had made it imperative for us to strengthen our army, that this was not in any way directed against France, and that it meant not so much overstraining our resources as turning them uniformly to account, and although even those with but slight knowledge of the facts could have had no doubt as to France's decision to increase her army having preceded ours, our action was indignantly discussed and misrepresented in France, where we were said to have aggressive designs on a peace-loving country whose population, and consequent defensive strength, was numerically far inferior to ours, and to have compelled it to make desperate exertions.

It was evident from the first that the new Army Bill would be strongly opposed in France, and that only very powerful means of influencing public opinion would avail to carry it through ; these means were therefore brought to bear to an extent and with a force, in the exercise of which French statesmen have shown themselves past masters from time immemorial. Other Ministers, indeed, besides the President, assured me that they did not misunderstand our military exertions, but the Government did nothing to guide the discussions in the Press and Parliament into more peaceful channels, let alone to make the Army Bill less rigorous. The Government was fully aware that it was a bold venture, and could not have failed to recognise the danger of the people finding the fresh personal and financial burden imposed on them so intolerable that sooner or later they might seek relief in a domestic upheaval, or reach the desperate conclusion that an " end with terror " would be preferable to " terror without end," but there was no going back now, the President's saying that " France must be strong " had to be made good, and Barthou and Millerand were the men to do this at any cost. It was only possible to do it by rousing passions against Germany, and thus one of those situations arose in which the sails of the French ship of State were filled with a stiff anti-German breeze.

The results soon became apparent, the tension of the atmosphere was relieved by a variety of

outbursts of French patriotism, the clamour for
Alsace-Lorraine again became insistent, the military
spirit asserted itself conspicuously, military shows
in the streets and on the stage, where the Germans
were invariably held up to scorn, increased in
number and were applauded, the well-known
literature of General Boulanger's day, which
carried on an infamous anti-German agitation,
was revived, and there were unfortunate incidents,
such as the ill treatment of harmless German
tourists at Nancy, the want of courtesy to German
airmen, who had made a compulsory landing
at Lunéville, etc. These incidents reacted on
our public opinion, whilst the French were furious
at the many and strong attacks made in our
Press on the Foreign Legion, all the more as
they laboured under the delusion that these attacks
were approved of, if not encouraged, by the
German Government.

Though the German public warnings against
joining the French Foreign Legion may have
been exaggerated here and there, they were on
the whole only too well justified. This applies
particularly to the way in which recruiting was
carried on by unscrupulous private individuals,
who deliberately evaded the regulations and took
shameful advantage of youthful inexperience.
Public discussion was not the proper way of
remedying this abuse, and it was impossible to
get it remedied through official channels, as the
French Government looked upon the matter as
an exclusively domestic concern, not open to
representations from outside. In spite of this,
we succeeded, by means of exceptionally cautious

private negotiations, in getting the worst of the abuses done away with, and a number of thought-less young Germans, who had been irregularly recruited, released from the obligations they had undertaken, thereby easing the situation. The Nancy and Lunéville incidents were also to some extent satisfactorily adjusted. An unexpected and unpleasant result of the German Press cam-paign against the Foreign Legion was that, instead of the rush of young Germans, whose adventurous ardour was unabated by the warn-ings, being stemmed, it increased to a degree never before attained. This was a very distressing state of affairs, which should give over-zealous patriots who pursue an aggressive foreign policy over the heads of their own Government, cause to reflect. The experience in the matter of the Foreign Legion is not the only case in which considerable harm has been done by inopportune procedure. More would be gained by leaving the official representatives of foreign policy to take the course which alone promises to achieve the desired end, after carefully considering the existing possibilities.

At the time when excitement ran high on both sides, I took an opportunity of represent-ing in a friendly way to the Premier, M. Barthou, that it was surely a very great pity that we should exhaust ourselves by mutually arming, and waste our energies in strife ; it would be more satisfactory to try to find some way of living peacefully alongside of one another, above all, by trying to calm down the excitement. With goodwill on both sides—and it was not lacking on our side—the goal appeared to me attainable. I made it quite clear that I was speaking on my own account, not acting on instructions in saying this, and did not want to enter into a great question. *" Rendez-nous l'Alsace-Lorraine, alors nous serons les meilleurs amis de la terre,"* M. Barthou replied with amazing candour, on which I immediately dropped the subject, the wiser for having learnt what value to attach to the wish, so frequently expressed by those in power in France, for an improvement in the Franco-German relations.

My giving a dinner at the Embassy in M. Poincaré's honour, in the midst of those far from pleasant times, in February 1914, made rather a sensation. It was the first time in the history of the third Republic that the President had been the guest of the German Ambassador ; hence it was, in a sense, an historical event which not a few thought might be a sign of a change for the better in Franco-German relations. Although I myself thought the fact of a courtesy which ignored political difficulties satisfactory, I could not share the opinion that it had a deeper political importance. M. Poincaré had taken quite a different line to his predecessors, and resolved on principle to accept invitations, particularly from foreign Ambassadors. He could not therefore refuse one from the German Embassy without its being painfully remarkable, any more than I could omit the invitation for my part. Moreover, the Kaiser had already broken the ice in Berlin by accepting an invitation from the French Ambassador, after the conclusion of the treaty over Morocco and the Congo.

The visit of the King and Queen of England
to Paris, in the spring of 1914, a solemn ratification in the eyes of all the world of the
close agreement which had been reached between
the two countries, was the crowning-point of
M'. Poincaré's success. It could not but be
obvious, even to those who knew very little
about it, that something important was in question,
for only State reasons could explain the decision
of Sir Edward Grey, the British Secretary of
State for Foreign Affairs, to accompany the Royal
couple to Paris himself, quite contrary to his
custom. The outward events were on the usual
lines ; even the after-dinner speeches, which
naturally laid stress on the friendship between
the two nations and pacific wishes, contained
nothing unusual. It was evident, from everything that took place, that the visit was not
to be regarded as a prelude to fresh agreements, but as an impressive ratification of what
had been agreed upon between England and
France. It did not appear to either of the
two parties expedient to give any detailed explanations with regard to these agreements ; they
were satisfied to show themselves to the world
hand in hand. It is true that, at Russia's
suggestion, advantage was taken of the presence
of the British Foreign Minister to draw the
English friend more closely than hitherto into
the Triple Entente : unquestionably with the consent of his Government, if not actually acting
on its instructions, M. Isvolsky submitted the
draft of an Anglo-Russian naval convention to
the British Minister, through the medium of

the French Minister for Foreign Affairs, M.
Doumergue, which mainly aimed at securing
English support for Russian military undertakings in the Baltic. Sir Edward Grey agreed
to the proposal without hesitation—and therewith
a further link was forged in the chain which
was to encircle Germany. That the convention
had not been finally concluded before the outbreak of war does not alter the fact that the
British Minister had agreed to it in principle.

A visit from the King and Queen of Denmark shortly afterwards had no political importance, except in so far as it gave the French
people reason to rejoice that the Republic had
managed to gain no small number of friendships.

A visit from the King of Serbia, a friend of
France, which might reasonably claim specially
friendly notice, in view of past events and
perhaps also of events to come, was in the
same category.

The reintroduction of three years' military service
having been decided upon in principle, after
extraordinarily violent parliamentary struggles, the
excitement somewhat died down. Those who
doubted whether the policy of a closely drawn
network of alliances and agreements, pursued by
the President and his Nationalistic following, was
consistent with the true interests of the French
people, who wanted rest and peace without all
too great sacrifices and obligations, again ventured
to express their views. That policy seemed to
them more calculated to intensify than to modify
the existing differences in Europe, and put
France in a position of dependence, which gave

cause for serious misgivings, particularly in view of the tendency to embark on new Slav adventures which was ever increasing in Russia. It would be well, they thought, for French policy to endeavour to relax the tension, so that the nation might be relieved of the frightful weight of the three years' military service as soon as possible. The President had not only to make a concession to this new feeling, a reaction as it were against the reaction, by appointing a Ministry under the prudent leadership of Doumergue, who numbered even political antagonists among his personal friends, but was also obliged to give way still further when the elections to the Chamber, in the spring of 1914, considerably strengthened the Radical and Socialist Left, thereby strengthening the opponents of the three years' military service and of the Nationalistic policy. After an abortive attempt to form a Government under Ribot, who was advanced in years and inclined to the Right, a Ministry was formed under the *bourgeois* Socialist, Vivani, who announced his intention of adhering to the Army Bill decided upon, but hinted at the possibility of its early revision.

The chances of more peaceful developments in France, and of this having an effect abroad, again seemed hopeful. There were signs, apparent to an attentive observer, that individual leading politicians were inclined to obviate the risks which had been increased by the military preparations on all sides, if not by openly leaning towards Germany, at all events by readiness to enter into an understanding with regard to individual questions outside the danger zone, as well as by adopting a less hostile tone in the Press and other organs of public opinion. This improved frame of mind facilitated and favoured negotiations between us and France over delimitation of the spheres of influence in Asia Minor and Syria, and the construction of railways in Asiatic Turkey. The inclination of the French Government to enter into agreements of this kind was considerably strengthened by the fact that we had entered into correspondence with the British Government with a similar object, and had been met in a way which not only gave reason to believe that the prospects of coming to an understanding in individual spheres of this kind were hopeful, but also that our general relations with England might very much improve. It almost looked as though the director of English foreign policy had misgivings as to the number of military agreements which had been concluded by the Triple Entente, and that he was now trying to relieve the strain.

Under these circumstances I thought it advisable to take a step towards improving the position myself, and having first obtained the Kaiser's consent and let M. Poincaré know of my intention, I suggested that M. Briand, the former Premier, should pay us an informal visit during the Kiel week. Prince Albert of Monaco kindly facilitated this by inviting 'Briand' to stay on board his yacht. No important political schemes of any kind were under consideration, it was merely a question of a casual meeting, which, in view of M. Briand's personality, might leave a pleasant and useful impression M. Briand seemed to like the idea, but he cancelled his acceptance of the invitation a few days later, on the ground of the claims made on his time by matters of domestic policy. The plan had been knocked on the head by the French Ambassador in St. Petersburg, M. Paléologue, President Poincaré's friend, who happened to be staying in Paris, and pointed out the danger of Kaiser Wilhelm's attractions.

In spite of the Western Powers' better frame of mind, the general situation still remained serious. The peace which had succeeded the Balkan Wars and the London Conference, rested on a fragile basis, and the extensive armament on all sides meant that combustible matter was being heaped up which might burst into a frightful conflagration on the first opportunity This opportunity was provided by the Serajevo murder and Austria-Hungary's ultimatum to Serbia.

The importance of the Serajevo incident was not fully realised by the French people in general. Apart from the fact of there being no monarchical feeling to wound, the scene of action was so distant as to be almost beyond the range of French *bourgeois* vision Besides this, other things engrossed their attention, above all, the sensational trial of Mme Caillaux, who had murdered the Editor of *Figaro*, M. Calmette. Calmette had been one of President Poincaré's most ardent champions, and consequently an opponent of Caillaux, whom he never tired of attacking in the most violent manner, even after the fall of his Government, and with such desperate weapons, in order to render him harmless, that Mme Caillaux, driven to desperation, shot him with a revolver. The trial, in which Caillaux's whole political and private life was ruthlessly dragged before the public, thus became, in the opinion of many onlookers, a bitter struggle between the Caillaux and Poincaré political parties, and everyone awaited the result with intense anxiety. The end of it was that Mme Caillaux was acquitted.

The demeanour of the Paris populace on the occasion of the great military review, which is always the principal feature of the National festival of July 14th, was characteristic of its frame of mind This institution is considered by those in power an excellent means of rousing the military spirit of the nation, and at the same time a standard by which to measure its patriotism. On this occasion colonial troops formed part of the pageant for the first time, particularly a battalion of fine picked Senegalese, the object being obviously to bring home to the people the extent and strength of the French fighting forces. The intended effect was achieved, all Paris streamed out to the review ground, applauded the show, and then gave itself up lightheartedly to further enjoyment of the national holiday, with the comfortable feeling that France's military strength was all that could be desired. It hardly occurred to anyone that events were brewing in the east of Europe which might put that strength to the test. The uncertainty of the European situation was indeed superficially recognised; people knew of an alliance and a friendship, and noticed how zealously they were cultivated by those in power, particularly by the President, but they had confidence in the defensive character of the agreements, which was always emphasised, and liked the brilliant pageants on the occasion of visits from the heads of friendly foreign States. They did not know how closely and menacingly the network of obligations had been drawn, how assiduously further knots had been tied, in the form of military and naval conventions and other preparations for war. Besides this, people were not in the habit of taking Press clamour seriously, and their confidence that the impending storm would disperse even now, as so often before, was not shaken. It was otherwise in the official world. Here, where what was going on was well known without being generally apparent, where the purport and importance of the existing agreements was understood, where every one must have been fully aware of the menacing bent of the driving forces in Russia, as well as of the military authorities in their own country, they could have been under no illusions as to the proximity and magnitude of the dangers, particularly as they had had no small share in piling up the material which gave cause for anxiety. They were, to all appearances, fully prepared, and ready for action.

The Vienna Government's excessively harsh ultimatum to Serbia revealed the seriousness of the position at a stroke. It was an absolute surprise even to me, personally, in so far as I had no knowledge whatever of what had taken place in the meantime. As recently as on the day on which the Note was forwarded, my Austro-Hungarian colleague had told me that, according to his information, it would be so worded that Serbia could agree to all the demands, and this would practically settle the matter. As is well known, we immediately followed up our ally's action by informing the Powers that we must consider the demand made by our allies for ample atonement and secure guarantees not only natural, but only too justifiable, and therefore we did not propose intervening in any way in the explanation between Vienna and Belgrade. It appeared of the utmost importance that the other Powers should also refrain from interfering, so as to avoid the possibility of complications arising which, in view of the existing obligations of alliance, might have incalculable consequences.

It may seem justifiable to ask whether such a communication to the Powers was necessary or advisable. Seeing how ready those in the camp of the Powers unfriendly to us always were to suspect all our political dealings, we had to reckon with the possibility that the step we were now taking might also be wrongly interpreted, that we might be credited with intentions of which we were in reality entirely innocent. The frank statement of our views and the suggestion that the conflict should be localised were certainly consistent with honourable intentions and a sincere wish to avoid complications which might lead to war between the Powers ; there was also good reason to hope that this object would be attained if all the

12

Powers put the amount of confidence in our proposal which it deserved. Most of the Powers were, however, inclined to pay less attention to the suggestion of localisation than to the disturbing fact of our having ' hastened to proclaim our attitude towards our ally so loudly, and laid such stress on the obligations of our alliance.

At that time the French Premier and Foreign Minister, Viviani, was on a visit to St Petersburg with the President of the Republic. Consequently, I had to deal with the Minister of Justice, Bienvenu Martin, who was representing him, as well as with the acting political Director, Berthelot, a man whose rôle was of special importance, on account of his more intimate acquaintance with the circumstances. My statements were not unfavourably received by the Minister He could only share the wish that the conflict should be localised, and was prepared to co-operate in that sense for the maintenance of peace. He could not, indeed, shut his eyes to the fact that it might not be easy for a Power like Russia, which had to reckon with strong Pan-Slav sympathies, to stand aside, particularly if Austria-Hungary were to insist on immediate and unconditional acceptance and fulfilment of what were, as regards several points, very far-reaching demands. The period of grace allowed to the Belgrade Government appeared to him too short, and as far as the tenor of the demands was concerned, there could be no doubt that some of them did not seem compatible with Serbia's sovereignty. The French

Government considered it a matter of course that Serbia must give ample satisfaction, must guarantee the punishment of crimes, and also give securities against further conspiracies being hatched. The Serbians had been advised from Paris to meet the Austro-Hungarian Government as far as they possibly could. But here again the French Government was of opinion that, in case of Serbia's not reservedly agreeing at once to all the demands, but wishing to negotiate over individual points, Austria-Hungary would do well not to reject this solution without further ado, provided Serbia's goodwill on the whole was evident, as it presumably would be.

In spite of its cautious wording and courteous tone, the Minister's answer made it clear that in case of a conflict, France would side with Russia. It was probably not given on the spur of the moment, but rather as the result of deliberations which had taken place in anticipation of an explicit demand being made by Austria-Hungary, and on the basis of information received and the views of the French representatives. On the other hand, our proposal that the conflict should be localised may have taken M. Bienvenu Martin by surprise, and if the French Government did not wish to incur the odium of being lacking in the "will to peace," it could not be rejected straightway. But the proposal lost the promised French support from the moment when M. Bienvenu Martin heard by telegram from M Viviani, who was on his way back from St. Petersburg, that in view of the probability of Austria-Hungary making harsh demands for satisfaction, the French and Russian Governments had agreed jointly to advise moderation in Vienna, and warn the Austro-Hungarian Government against threatening Serbia. The very interference on the part of the Powers we were trying to avoid! In this connection it is significant that the fact of our " localisation " proposal having been assented to in the first instance, is suppressed in the French Yellow Book.

The Austro - Hungarian ultimatum was immediately discussed in the French Press, and severely condemned. It was evident that Austria-Hungary was forcing war, which she thought she needed as a diversion from her domestic confusion and strife ; to all appearance Germany was backing her up in this, as it was hardly conceivable that the Vienna Government would have taken such a serious step without being in close touch with Berlin. The moment may have seemed favourable to both Powers for action on an imposing scale, when England was taken up with the Ulster crisis, Russia was crippled by labour disturbances, France's military preparations, according to M. Humbert's revelations, did not seem to be complete, and when, in addition to this, it might be assumed that the absence of the President and the Premier would cause some confusion.

As a result of one of the indiscretions which are common in Paris, the Press was immediately informed of my statement to the French Government, and made the most reckless statements and misstatements, going even so far as to assert that it was a case of a thinly-veiled threat, against which a very decided protest must be made. I protested strongly to the French Government at once against the indiscretion, and the misrepresentation of what I had said, and, acting on instructions received, I stated definitely that the German Government had had nothing whatever to do with drafting the ultimatum to Serbia, although, on its publication, they recognised the demand for satisfaction as justifiable. Strange to say, I was assured that the Government had had nothing to do with the indiscretion, which they regretted, and steps would be taken to calm down the Press Nevertheless, the impression I gained on this occasion was that the views held at the Quai d'Orsay were not very different to those of the Press; anyhow, our communication was looked upon as an action less likely to have a reassuring effect than to cause anxiety. In spite of a semi-official notice, and although I took some trouble to try to convince the Press myself that there was no question of a harsh wording of the Note forwarded to Belgrade having been agreed upon between Vienna and Berlin, the Press persisted in its opinion, all the more as it professed to know that our communication had only been made in Paris, not elsewhere. It must, therefore, be regarded as a serious warning addressed to France. Individual Nationalistic newspapers even spoke of an outrageous attempt to intimidate.

In the meantime the Russian Government had made the momentous announcement to the Powers, and at the same time to the public, that the

Serbo-Austrian conflict could not be a matter of indifference to it.   Almost simultaneously it became known that Russia was already taking military measures.   This attitude on the part of Russia, which had necessarily to be regarded, like our "localisation" proposal, as a threat, but with far more reason, made the position extremely serious; the Serbo-Austrian became a European question, which was what we had tried to avoid. If the cause of peace was not to be lost, it was necessary that efforts should be made without delay to induce Russia to pause in the dangerous course on which she had embarked.   An effort in this direction could only be made, with any hope of success, by her French ally, and it seemed to be facilitated by the fact that the Vienna Government had hastened to explain in St Petersburg that it did not contemplate any territorial gain in Serbia, and would not break up the Kingdom.   Accordingly, I was instructed to urge the French Government, "with whom we know we are in agreement in wishing to maintain European peace," to exert its influence in St. Petersburg   The result of the steps taken in consequence of this was, unfortunately, far from satisfactory.   M. Bienvenu Martin, indeed, assured me that the appeal for solidarity in desiring peace made a good impression, and would be given the consideration it deserved; but, as regards exerting influence in St. Petersburg, he was evasive, if he did not absolutely refuse the request. He would not say "No," but thought an effort on the part of the Powers to exert a restraining influence in Vienna would be opportune   The

Vienna Government would do well to show itself open to negotiations, Serbia having apparently yielded on almost every point. Moreover, he pointed out that he must first communicate with the Prime Minister, who was on his way back from St. Petersburg, as to the answer to be given on behalf of the French Government I did not omit to object that the Minister's idea that the Powers should exert their joint influence in Vienna did not seem compatible with the view on which we had insisted from the beginning, that Austria-Hungary and Serbia should be left alone.

A private conversation with the acting political Director, Berthelot, gave me a deeper insight into the ideas which prevailed at the Quai d'Orsay. In view of the previous indiscretion, and in order to avoid fresh misrepresentations, I suggested that a report should be sent to the Press of my second interview with the Minister, in which mention should be made of the solidarity of the wish for peace. M. Berthelot thought this going too far, and only agreed to a communication being sent to the Press which said very little. Moreover, he did not disguise the fact that he himself took the view that we were egging on our ally, and "wanted war." Although our assurance that we had not been aware of the text of the Austro-Hungarian Note to Serbia before its publication, must be respected, still, he was bound to believe that the Vienna Government could not have taken so unusual a step without our fore-knowledge and approval Our refusal to advise moderation in Vienna now was remarkable, seeing that Serbia had as good as entirely given in, and our warning against joint representations in Vienna strengthened the view that we were adopting the position of defending our ally against the other Powers. As far as the request that France should make cautious efforts to exert influence in Russia was concerned, M. Viviani, whose decision must be asked, would in all probability instruct him to say that France would be prepared to do this, but only on condition that we should do the same in Vienna. I insisted, for my part, that we could not strike down our ally's arm, which she had raised in order to obtain satisfaction for a frightful crime, and to defend herself against dangers which seriously menaced her existence and indirectly affected us, too. The view spread by Russia, that Austria-Hungary wanted to " destroy " Serbia was incorrect; we had no reason for trying to dissuade our ally from intentions which did not exist. The turn things had taken made St. Petersburg the centre where every possible effort must be made to maintain peace. Personally, however, I thought it not impossible that the Vienna Government might be open to suitable suggestions which did not savour in any way of pressure I must protest strongly against the view that our attitude gave reason to believe that we wanted war. No impartial observer could look upon the proposal to localise the conflict, the suggestion that cautious efforts should be made to influence St. Petersburg, and the appeal to our solidarity with France in wishing for peace, as acts indicating a desire to disturb peace. They were, on the contrary, clear indications of a desire to safeguard peace.

M. Berthelot's remarks, which at all events had the merit of being candid, are characteristic of the views which obtained in Paris from the beginning. We were not only accused, as a matter of course, of having kindled the conflagration, but were also saddled with the odium of having fanned the flames instead of trying to extinguish them. This tendency was conspicuous in the Yellow Book, published immediately after the outbreak of war, in which reports and information, even from interested sources, whose object was to prove that a desire for war had got the upper hand in Germany and Austria, and to represent us as the driving force behind our ally, and twist almost every step we took into the reverse of its real object, were quoted *ad libitum*. Thus, the proposal of " localisation " was interpreted as an attempt to guard against the Powers exerting influence in Vienna, the suggestion that they should make representations in St. Petersburg and the appeal to the French desire for peace, as a clumsy manœuvre to sow dissension between France and Russia. Moreover, the similarity between M. Berthelot's view and the attitude of the Paris Press is remarkable. It is also remarkable that the Yellow Book, so voluble in complaints of our behaviour, is silent when it is a question of unmistakable efforts we made to solve the problem peaceably. For instance, it contains no reference whatever to a conversation I had with the Permanent Under-Secretary in the Foreign Office,

M. Abel Ferry, in which I again urged counsels
of moderation in St. 'Petersburg, and at the
same time hinted that we should not absolutely
dissociate ourselves from friendly suggestions in
Vienna which did not exert pressure. In order
to dispel the French distrust, I went so far as
to offer at the same time to urge my Government
to act with France in Vienna and St. Petersburg.
It was all of no avail, the prejudice in French
responsible quarters was too strong to be uprooted.

No answer was given by M. Viviani as regards
the step we asked France to take in St. Petersburg,
at all events I was not informed of it, although
he was in constant communication with Paris.
This put the refusal beyond doubt. The question
whether the attitude of the French Government
would have been different, if M. Viviani had
been amongst his peace-loving Party friends, and
not pre-eminently under the influence of the impressions gained in St. Petersburg, is difficult
to answer, but may nevertheless be asked. In
any case, by refusing to warn St Petersburg
in good time against further disastrous action,
the French Government incurred a considerable
share of responsibility for the breakdown of the
peace efforts. A warning against precipitancy
in St. Petersburg was only uttered when the
disaster was already in full swing, and even
then only half-heartedly, clearly hinting that it
was advisable not to give Germany any " pretext " for taking military measures. There is
no doubt that the attitude of the French Government was strongly influenced by Isvolsky, who
continued to insist, regardless of the definite

statement made by the Vienna Government that
it was not seeking territorial gain and would
not encroach on the existence of the Kingdom
of Serbia, that Russia could not permit Serbia's
" destruction "—*écrasement*.

The further negotiations concerned Sir Edward
Grey's proposal of an Ambassadors' Conference, an
instrument of mediation which had proved its
value in the Albanian dispute. The idea met
with approval at once in Paris, but we objected
that it would have an inherent tendency to put
pressure on Austria-Hungary. As a matter of
fact, Vienna was unwilling to agree to the proposal. We, on the other hand, showed ourselves
favourably disposed towards a further proposal
made by the British Foreign Minister, namely,
that the Vienna Government should be satisfied
with Serbia's reply, or accept it as a basis for
further negotiations. But in spite of our recommending it, the Vienna Government was not prepared to agree to this either. Our efforts were
then directed towards paving a way, to frank
discussion between Vienna and St. Petersburg.
They had some result, but were overtaken and
foiled by Russia and France's military preparations It also appears doubtful whether they would
have effected any essential change in the course of
events, England having made it perfectly clear both
in Paris and in St. Petersburg that, in case
of the negotiations breaking down, she could
be relied on to act with her friends. This gave
a disastrous stimulus to the " will for war,"
which had undoubtedly existed for long past in
St. Petersburg.

In this connection mention must be made of the fact that Russia not only made extensive military preparations which manifested a "will to war," but, as became known later on, had taken the most momentous decisions months before. The following conclusion had been reached at a Cabinet Council : " The time for the attainment of the goal is approaching. It can only be attained by war. It is the business of the Minister for Foreign Affairs to create favourable prior conditions." This was the text of the protocol of the Cabinet Council meeting, this was the Russian desire for peace, this was the Russian policy of which President Poincaré could hardly have been in ignorance when he was staying in St. Petersburg shortly before the war broke out. And an admission made by M. Paléologue, the French Ambassador in St. Petersburg, in his memoirs, shows plainly how it was pursued. He speaks of having met the English Ambassador in Sazonov's ante-room, and of how the Ambassador, who had just been with Sazonov, whispered to him : " Russia is determined to go to war. We must, therefore, saddle Germany with the whole responsibility and initiative of the attack ; this will be the only way of winning over public opinion in England to the war. I earnestly beg you to help to influence M. Sazonov in this sense." [1]

[1] The actual words used by M Paléologue in his book, *La Russie des Tsars pendant la Grande Guerre*, are as follows .—

" La situation a encore empiré. . . . Je ne doute plus que la Russie ne marche au fond ; she is thoroughly in earnest Je viens de supplier Sazonov de ne consentir à aucune mesure militaire que l'Allemagne pourrait interpréter comme une provocation. Il

This request was hardly needed, seeing that
M. Paléologue had been indefatigable in calling the attention of the Russian Ministers, even
indeed of the Tsar, to the dangers which were
alleged to be menacing Russia from Germany,
in a way which cannot be described otherwise
than as inciting her to go to war

Preparations had been going on quietly for
some time past, not only in Russia, but also
in France, with a view to warlike developments.
As far back as in the winter of 1913–14
provision was made for supplying Paris with
large stores of flour, at the suggestion of the
military authorities. Stress was laid on its being
a matter of urgency. " Time presses," said the
Governor of Paris, General Michel, in January
1914; " this is an unusual year, we cannot tell
what it may bring us. We cannot tell whether
we shall have mobilisation in March or April ! "
These preparations might possibly be regarded
as precautionary measures, but other steps taken
by the French Government were even more
suspicious. It approached the Swiss Federal
Council in the spring, offering to supply Switzerland with wheat in case of war, which was
spoken of as imminent and inevitable. France,
it said, did not desire war, but the day of
reckoning with regard to Alsace-Lorraine was
at hand. France thought it right to secure
Switzerland the supply of wheat, as the usual

faut laisser au gouvernement allemand toute la responsabilité et
toute l'initiative de l'attaque L'opinion anglaise n'admettra l'idée
de participer à la guerre que si l'aggression vient indubitablement
de l'Allemagne . . De grâce, parlez dans le même sens à Sazonov
—Je ne lui tiens pas d'autre langage "—C V.

delivery via Rotterdam would not be possible in case of war—a significant reference to the blockade. On the outbreak of war between Austria and Serbia, the 14th Army Corps manœuvres were immediately broken off, all officers of the Army and Navy were ordered to rejoin their formations and ships by July 27th, steps were also taken to arm the fortresses and' place other positions in a state of readiness, and troops were brought from Morocco and Algiers.

I was now instructed to speak to the Premier, who had in the meantime returned from St. Petersburg, about the French military preparations, and to point out most emphatically that such steps would compel us to take corresponding 'defensive' measures. We should have to proclaim the "state of imminent danger of war," and though this would not mean calling out the reserves, or mobilisation, it would have the effect of increasing the tension. We still continued to hope for the maintenance of peace. M. Viviani did not deny that a few military measures had been taken, but he said it was solely a case of precautionary measures of insignificant extent, and which were being carried out unostentatiously. There was no question at all of mobilisation. He would not personally feel uneasy if we were to do the same, although he would think this a pity, on account of the alarming effect on public opinion. He thought the best means of averting further nervous agitation would be to mediate as soon as possible, no matter in what form. He, too, would not abandon the hope of peace, which people in France sincerely wished' to preserve. The very same day, as the Yellow Book shows, the Minister, acting on the tendency to make us appear the peace-breakers, forwarded an enumeration of German and French military measures to London, with the object of proving that in this respect France had only slowly and hesitatingly followed our example. It has become evident, however, from later publications, that in order not to give us the start of her "under the pretext of danger of war," France had already taken far-reaching precautions at a time when a "state of danger of war" had not yet been proclaimed in Germany; on the contrary, it had only been pointed out to France that if her preparations continued, we should be compelled to make the proclamation.

Things now took a tempestuous and disastrous course. Sincerely desiring to leave no stone unturned to save the peace which was already imperilled, the German Government had strongly advised Vienna to endeavour to reach an understanding with Russia, and had achieved this aim, not without difficulty. We had further stated our assent in principle to Sir Edward Grey's proposal of mediation jointly with England, Italy and France, and had also said that the Serbian reply Note seemed to us a suitable basis for negotiations. That did not prevent M. Viviani's saying in a circular Note to the French Ambassadors that Germany's attitude seemed to demonstrate conclusively that she intended humiliating Russia, breaking up the Triple Entente, and, if that were unattainable, going to war.

Our efforts to bring Vienna and St. Petersburg

together were still going on, and did not appear hopeless, when the Russian Government followed the partial mobilisation against Austria-Hungary by a general mobilisation of her Army and Navy against us, in spite of the most urgent representations from our Ambassador in St. Petersburg, regardless of the Kaiser's repeated affecting appeals to the Tsar's friendship, prudence, and love of peace, and of the Tsar's efforts to stop the mobilisation. Not only this, but it was a flagrant breach of the word of honour given by Russian statesmen. The attitude of the French Government was very different to ours. No urgent representation in St. Petersburg, no telegram from the President to the Tsar, nothing but belated and equivocal advice not to give Germany any " excuse " for mobilising, when the harm was already being done. On the contrary, Russia was repeatedly assured that she could not only rely on France's diplomatic support, but on her fulfilling all the obligations arising out of her alliance. Besides this, President Poincaré wrote to the King of England, with the evident object of inducing England to abandon her cautious attitude of hesitation.

On July 31st, I was instructed to inform the French Premier that Russia's mobilisation had compelled us to proclaim a " state of impending danger of war," which must be followed by mobilisation, unless Russia suspended all her military measures against us within twelve hours. Mobilisation would inevitably mean war ; I was therefore to ask whether France would remain neutral in a Russo-German war The answer was to be given within eighteen hours. The instructions further stated that in case of France promising to remain neutral, which was unlikely, a guarantee was to be given, in the form of conceding us a right to occupy 'the fortresses of Toul and Verdun for the duration of the war with Russia.

In the conversation I had with M. Viviani, on the evening of July 31st, he professed, to my surprise, to have no information of a Russian general mobilisation against us, and said he only knew of a partial mobilisation against Austria-Hungary and general precautionary measures. He would not abandon hope that the worst might yet be avoided. On my pointing out that not only the whole Russian army, but the fleet had also been mobilised, a clear proof that the measure was directed against us, M. Viviani could make no reply. He promised to give an answer to the question of neutrality the next afternoon, after the Cabinet Council. His ignorance of the Russian general mobilisation seems very remarkable, in view of the fact that it had been publicly proclaimed in the early morning of that day in St. Petersburg, had been ordered the evening before, and undoubtedly decided on even earlier; further, in view of the close relationship of alliance, and finally of the circumstance that the Premier had just returned from St. Petersburg, and therefore ought not to have been in ignorance of what was intended there. It must either be assumed that he knew all about it or that the Russian Government had misled him in the same way as it had tried to mislead our representatives in St Petersburg. On the other hand, it is certain that the French

Ambassador in St. Petersburg had been specially informed by the Russian Government of the decision to order general mobilisation, on the evening of July 29th—he confirms this himself in his publications.

Paris could not be in any doubt that the Russian mobilisation was equivalent to war, all the less, as this was a principle on which stress had been laid when concluding the alliance. In the course of the night M. Viviani telegraphed to St. Petersburg that he proposed merely answering my enquiry as to neutrality by saying that France would be guided by her own interests. France did not owe an account of her actions to any one but her ally. If the French official reports published of the interview represent that my question only extended to "France's attitude," that is misleading. In reality, what I said was, that after the Russian mobilisation and our ultimatum, which probably would not be accepted, our decision now depended mainly on France's attitude, as to which I therefore asked for a statement. If France decided on adopting a neutral attitude, we should be prepared to do the same, further details could then be discussed. Of course, I did not allude in any way to making over the fortresses as a guarantee, as this question could only arise in case of the French answer being in the affirmative. The answer was given the next day, August 1st, before the expiration of the eighteen hours, and was as follows : " France will do what her interests demand." M. Viviani could not be induced to give any explanation. On the other hand, he

said, apparently in order to justify the vague-
ness of the answer, that he had reason to believe
the general situation had changed and was considerably easier. Russia had accepted in principle
a fresh proposal made by Sir Edward Grey as to
the suspension of military preparations all round,
and negotiations, and Austria-Hungary had again
expressly stated that she would not encroach
on the Serbian territorial *status* and Serbian
sovereignty. This revived the hope of a peaceable settlement which had already been abandoned.

I had heard nothing from Berlin of this fresh
proposal, and was therefore not in a position to say
anything definite. I never for a moment doubted
that the answer to the question as to neutrality was
a refusal, in spite of its being so indefinite ;
I also told M. Viviani at once, without his con-
tradicting me, that I took it to be in the
negative, and that my Government would probably
do the same. There was consequently no object
in raising the question of the fortresses. It
is obvious that the idea was not a happy one.
From a purely military standpoint the demand
for a guarantee of neutrality may be correct,
from a political point of view it was a mistake. As matters stood, France's neutrality would
have been such an immense advantage to us
that we should have had more reason for offering than for demanding something for its maintenance. Moreover, the demand showed a lack
of correct appreciation of French national sentiment. If the French had even for only a passing
moment thought of agreeing to the proposal of
neutrality, the demand for the surrender of their

most important fortresses would have nipped any
understanding in the bud. The *faux pas* can
only be accounted for by assuming that the
demand for a guarantee in such a form must
have been urged on those responsible for our
foreign policy by parties with no political training, and that the reason for not refusing it was
only the certainty that France's attitude would
make it useless to raise the question, which
was, in fact, the case. After trying for years to
decipher the telegraphic instructions concerning
the surrender of the fortresses, the French at
last succeeded, and they made capital out of
this discovery by professing to regard it as
further proof that we wished for war. This interpretation of it seems absolutely arbitrary. The
idea of asking that the fortresses should be
surrendered was not the result of a desire to
bring about a rupture under any circumstances,
but of a mistaken calculation.

The order for French mobilisation was given
at 3.40 p.m., Paris time, on the same day as
the answer as to France's attitude, twenty minutes
before the German order. It seems important to
give the exact hour, because it is asserted on the
French side that the French mobilisation was
in consequence of ours. On this I immediately
called on the Premier again, in order to make
another effort to obtain a more definite statement, but I had no success. M. Viviani said
he could not change the ˏformula in which he
had given me his answer at midday. As regards
the mobilisation just ordered, he said it did
not by any means point to aggressive intentions,

and that this would be emphasised in a proclamation. There was consequently, nothing to prevent conciliatory negotiations being continued on the basis of Sir Edward Grey's latest proposal, to which France had agreed, and which she warmly supported. Steps had been taken by the French to prevent collisions on the frontier by ordering the maintenance of an intervening zone of ten kilometres wide.

It is evident, from the official French publications as to the critical days before the war, that M. Viviani was rather uneasy at my having alluded to the possibility of my taking my departure, after the refusal of neutrality. He thought this gentle hint might be considered a proof that we were bent on a rupture and on war under any circumstances. It was also said that I had already had the Embassy archives brought into safety. This was quite a wrong interpretation of what I had said, and was due, like many other misrepresentations, to the persistent French efforts to saddle us in the eyes of the public with the odium of breaking the peace. M. Viviani overlooks the fact that, in giving this hint, I had in view the possibility that the hostility of the Paris populace, which had already obliged me to shelter the staffs of the Embassy and consulate and their families in the Embassy, as well as other fellow countrymen who were subjected to annoyance, might at any moment assume a form which would necessitate a hasty departure. There was no foundation whatever for the statement that the Embassy archives had been brought into safety.

Up to the moment of mobilisation, the French populace had been in a highly nervous, but taking the excitable French temperament into consideration, fairly peaceable frame of mind on the whole. Resentment and animosity had been shown towards Germans, but nothing was known of any more serious excesses. Under the influence of the Government, and thanks also to my exertions, the language of the Press had been in general moderate. Confidence was frequently expressed that, in view of the close agreement between the Entente Powers, Germany would not venture on extremes. Importance was also attached to Grey's fresh proposal of mediation. Forces by no means to be despised were secretly occupied in trying to calm down the people and the Government, first and foremost among them the influential Socialist leader and enthusiastic champion of international peace, Jaurès. The indefatigable activity of this remarkable man, who had fathomed the Russo-French intrigues years before, and had the courage to show them up, who also did not hesitate to point to the Russian Ambassador, Isvolsky, as the instigator of the war, was brought to an end, on the day of mobilisation, by the hand of an assassin. The deed of blood has remained for years unaccounted for and unexpiated, to all appearance because the trial threatened to bring things to light which would impair the *Union Sacrée,* and rouse popular indignation against the rulers. The *Vox populi* had at once pointed to the Nationalists as having, figuratively speaking if not actually, " pressed the weapon into the assassin's hand."

On the very night of that day, the momentous news arrived that we had replied to the Russian challenge by declaring war. All hope of avoiding the worst now vanished into thin air, a clear *casus fœderis* had arisen for France. Had this not been the case, possibly the murder of Jaurès might have led to a popular agitation which would have obliged the Government to be cautious. But now it was obvious to every one that we had given the signal for a settlement of the dispute by force of arms, and that war between France and Germany had become inevitable. Public excitement was turned in this direction, and it was easy for the Nationalists to encourage it. From that moment it took the form of furious resentment against us, first and foremost against the Kaiser, who had authorised letting loose the dogs of war. The fury was all the greater against the Kaiser, because not a few had been pleased to look up to him as a sure bulwark of peace, and were now disappointed in a way which seemed intolerable to their *amour propre* The result was that there were innumerable outbreaks of hatred against everything that was or seemed to be German, as well as acts of violence which added fuel to the flame.

The following day, August 3rd, I had another interview with the Premier, who did not disguise the fact that the position was serious, but still showed some confidence that Grey's proposal might yet save it. Events, however, were already taking their irresistible course. I had had to inform M. Viviani of our invasion of Luxemburg, and explain that it was not a hostile action, measures were merely being taken to safeguard the railways under German administration. In the evening I received a communication from the French Government, protesting against isolated instances of Germans having crossed the frontier, and of hostile acts which had led to bloodshed. These occurrences, apparently foolish enterprises embarked on by small German reconnoitring parties, were reported in the French Press with the usual exaggerations as serious hostile movements which we had commenced without any declaration of war, and roused the excitement of the people to fever heat, as was proved by the innumerable cases of Germans being ill treated. There were also noisy demonstrations against the German Embassy, which, however, were suppressed.

On the afternoon of August 3rd, just when the tension was at its height, a telegram in cipher arrived with the Imperial Chancellor's signature, a sign that it concerned a matter of special importance. There was no doubt in my mind that its contents would be decisive. Unfortunately, the telegram was so mutilated that, in spite of every effort, only fragments of it could be deciphered. It was clear, however, that air attacks had been made by the French on Nuremberg, Karlsruhe, and Wesel, that I was to ask for my passports at 6 o'clock, to hand over the Germans to the protection of the American Ambassador, and leave. There was no time to make any enquiry as to the illegible part. As I knew from other sources that we felt bound to declare war in consequence of a French air attack on Nuremberg, I had to make up my mind to fall back on the little that could be clearly understood from the telegram, to justify the declaration of war. The illegible part of the telegram, as I learnt later on, concerned not inconsiderable French hostile movements on the Alsace frontier, which had been crossed by detachments of troops in close order, in spite of the promised ten kilometre zone. It was only when the war had been going on for some time that the statements as to French air attacks proved to have been based on disastrous mistakes. They seem to have been merely the product of highly overwrought imagination. How such false reports could have been given the weight of facts in our responsible quarters, and indeed of such momentous facts, is inconceivable. As far as the question of French detachments having crossed the frontier is concerned, a question to which I was unable to make any reference in my last communication to the French Government, owing to extraneous circumstances, we have established this so incontestably that French denials cannot alter the fact. An adverse fate had, however, obliged me to confine myself to statements which gave the French Government abundant ground for asserting that we had trumped up excuses to justify our attack. Not only the Press, but also Ministers, and particularly M. Poincaré, have delighted in making use of this effective means of proving that we made an unprovoked attack.

The Premier Viviani, to whom I first conveyed the declaration of war by word of mouth, to be followed immediately by a written announcement, received it without any sign of emotion, somewhat as a matter of course. But he most emphatically declined to accept the reason given for it. He said at once that it was out of the question that any of the air attacks spoken of could actually have taken place. I had not omitted to mention that, in consequence of the telegram having been so mutilated, a considerable part of the instructions which had reached me were indecipherable, and presumably concerned French hostilities elsewhere. I had to take further advantage of this last opportunity, to make a complaint. As I was starting for the Ministry, a man jumped on to the footboard of my motor in front of the Embassy and forced his way into it, gesticulating wildly, and using threatening language ; he was immediately followed by a second. As I was alone, I had to invoke the help of the police stationed at the street corner to get rid of the intruders. Two other men then got into the vehicle, and a third seated himself beside the chauffeur. They explained that they were detectives by whispering the word "*service*." They then remained at hand with loaded revolvers till the moment of my getting into the train, and behaved admirably. M. Viviani expressed due regret for the occurrence.

I feel it necessary to lay stress on this unimportant incident, because the Paris Press absolutely misrepresented it, and said that, during the last critical days, I had driven remarkably often through the streets, as many as five times in one day, undoubtedly with the intention of exposing myself to personal attack, and making the attack a pretext for breaking off negotiations, as I was hard up for one. The simple truth is that, during those sad days, I never left the Embassy except for the purpose of my visits to the Premier. On the other hand, my motor often went out either empty or with one of the Embassy staff, to bring distressed fellow-countrymen under the sheltering roof of the Embassy, or to procure food for the innumerable other German refugees I had taken in. No less an individual than M. Poincaré gave credence to the invention, as foolish as it is malicious, of the provocation I had given, and related it repeatedly, once in a solemn speech to a select audience on the national holiday, July 14, 1915, a second time, in a lecture on the origin of the war, long after it, and on this occasion with all sorts of embellishments. I had to bring the matter forward in public in order to obtain a withdrawal of the statement. M. Viviani was also fond of relating legends of this kind. The French Press was also able to report—thanks to the usual indiscretions—that I was visibly affected on the occasion of my last interview, and again M. Poincaré did not scruple to say that this was due to the embarrassment I felt in telling an untruth about the air attacks. I willingly admit that I did not appear indifferent when making the declaration of war, but of course this was not because I felt ashamed of telling an untruth, as I could not know that it was so at ·the time. I felt the tremendous weight of the mission with which I was charged, and do not envy M.

Viviani the icy composure he maintained. We took leave of one another with suitable gravity, but with perfect courtesy. Having earnestly recommended the Germans I was leaving behind me in France, thousands of whom were homeless, to M. Viviani's humanity, and received a promise to provide for them at once, and having then discussed my journey, I was able to say, as my last word, that I was conscious of having honestly endeavoured to establish cordial relations with France and done everything in my power to avert the disastrous turn things had now taken. I looked on the coming war as the greatest misfortune that could befall mankind.

The question of how the innumerable Germans in France could be saved from sad fates was one of great anxiety. Apart from chance visitors their number would amount to about 150,000 in France, in Paris alone to 80,000. There was reason to believe that, in case of war, the French Government would not turn out all the Germans as in 1870, but would be more likely to intern them, particularly those fit for military service. As it was to be expected that when mobilisation began passenger traffic between France and other countries would be completely suspended, provision had to be made for Germans, by their official representative, by inducing them to leave in good time, and helping them to do so. The first thing considered was, therefore, the possibility of warning them of the dangers impending. There were immediately found to be considerable difficulties of various kinds in the way of this. First of all the date. So long as efforts to preserve peace were going on and were not altogether hopeless—and they were continued up to the last—an official warning did not seem expedient; in the first place because it would have torn many Germans, probably most of them, from lucrative positions and existences they had toiled to build up, and might give occasion for complaint, and claims for compensation, in case of the worst being averted, and then, a still more important consideration, because such a measure would have had a most alarming effect, and would certainly have been pointed to by the French as proof of the German "will to war." Why, even the mere fact of my having quietly made a few travelling arrangements for myself and the Embassy staff had been sufficient to cause not only the Press but also the French Government to make the audacious assertion that I looked on war as inevitable "because we wanted it."

Under these circumstances there could be no question of anything but cautious warnings *sub rosa*. But here again a difficulty arose from the fact that the great majority of our fellow-countrymen were either not within reach or not known to the Embassy and the consulates. Only relatively few were in touch with the official representations in times of peace; there was no legal compulsion in this respect. In spite of this, no stone was left unturned to give warning in good time and to as many as possible. Instructions were hastily given to the consulates at the seaports to warn captains of German ships. As soon as the serious turn things were taking became evident, Germans making enquiries at the Embassy and the consulates were given to understand that, although the position was not hopeless as yet, it was serious, and that those who were in an independent position would do well to leave without attracting attention. A few days afterwards, all were urgently advised to leave. Simultaneously with the order for French mobilisation, an order was issued by the President of the French Republic, which only gave the Germans one day's grace in which to leave the country, after which they would be interned. Moreover, it is significant that this decree applied to Austrians and Hungarians as well, but not to Italians, a sign that such of the Powers were reckoned upon as did in fact come into the war immediately, just as upon the war itself. In individual places this order was given out before the proper date, from which it is evident that the French Government had long since made far-reaching preparations, when they were still pretending to have been absolutely taken by surprise by the events.

After the publication of this order, provision had to be made for our fellow-countrymen by providing them with the means and opportunity of leaving, both difficult matters, as sufficient money could no longer be procured and only a few trains to Belgium and Switzerland were available. But even these difficulties were overcome by the most strenuous exertions. Many thousands of Germans, above all, those of military age, were helped to get home in this way, and the distress of those remaining behind was to some extent alleviated. Scanty accommodation could be provided in the Embassy for no small number of Germans who were rendered homeless, until the evening of August 3rd, when all official activity came to an abrupt end with the breaking off of negotiations. The only thing I could still do for my afflicted fellow-countrymen was to ask the Premier personally to provide for them, and to entrust their further protection to the American Ambassador, who readily undertook it.

Many Germans did not attach due importance to the warning they received, and either did not consider there was any hurry to leave, or else made extensive preparations which delayed them, and consequently missed the moment when it would have been possible to make the journey. The stoppage of all railway communication on the evening of August 2nd took them by surprise, and they had to remain in France, where, contrary to all justice and humanity, and in spite of the explicit promises given by the French Government, they were treated as prisoners long after the time when the reopening of railway communication would have enabled them to return home. The hardship of this pitiable fate was increased in the great majority of cases by the most abominable and degrading treatment. Under these circumstances it is easy to understand those arbitrarily detained in France, and their despairing relatives, having here and there expressed indignation, and complained of the supposed insufficient provision made for them by their official representatives. This was pardonable. But that others, presumably infected by the widespread tendency to run down their foreign representatives, should have openly complained of insufficient provision, without full knowledge or enquiry, is very deplorable.

The departure from Paris took place very quietly from a station near the Embassy, late in the evening of the day on which war was declared, and without any *contretemps*. The fact that the special train intended for me and my party had been in readiness long before I asked to be given facilities for leaving throws a remarkable light on the concern M. Viviani expressed with regard to my travelling arrangements. I did not know which way we were going. I had naturally asked to be sent the shortest way to the German frontier, possibly in the Strasbourg direction, but had been met by the objection that the line was already closed by German military measures, and that we should have to go by another route. I was given no escort, and the railway officials said they did not know which way we should go. The end of it was that we started for Cologne via Belgium. At the Belgian frontier, however, I was told that the train could not go on to Cologne, as the tunnels and bridges were destroyed. I had no knowledge whatever of our having broken off relations with Belgium that night, nor did I even know there had been any such intention. Even as Secretary of State, not a word had ever been said to me by the military authorities of plans of the kind, although they had undoubtedly existed for long past. On the contrary,

all I knew was that Belgian neutrality, of which
Germany was one of the guarantors, was considered inviolable, and that assurances to that
effect had repeatedly been given in Brussels.
Our military attaché in Paris, a General Staff
officer who had formerly been attached to the
Embassy in Brussels, had also assured me that
if any question of a march through Belgium
should arise, it would only be later on. As
things had turned out, I was in danger of
being taken prisoner in Belgium, with whom we
were now at war, if not of experiencing a
worse fate, with the many persons accompanying
me, including not a few officers. That we escaped
this is perhaps only due to the fact that we travelled
through Belgium by night. With some difficulty,
the train was finally taken via Brussels and Ant-
werp through Holland to the German frontier, which
we reached at Goch.

At this juncture it seems opportune to cast a
glance back at several points in my recent experiences, which are of considerable importance
in forming an opinion of the success or failure
of diplomacy. The fact that I had no knowledge whatever of what was going on when,
in the course of my journey, I reached Belgium,
with whom we were already at war, is instructive
to those who are wont to form adverse opinions
of the higher diplomatic representatives, in the
belief that they hold the reins of high policy
in their hands. This is a mistaken belief, as
is clearly shown by my case. The example proves
that not only is the representative's sphere of
influence, but also his range of vision, so limited

14

that he has no knowledge of events which are tantamount to a political upheaval. It proves at the same time that those who direct the policy may pursue disastrous courses, not of their own will, but under strong pressure from other authorities, who are consequently responsible.

The demand that France should surrender important fortresses, as a guarantee of her neutrality, is a no less instructive incident—an attempt to secure her neutrality by absolutely futile methods. Had I been placed in the position which would have obliged me to make this demand, in accordance with my instructions, it would have been the worst mistake I could have made, although I should not have been personally to blame, for the war with France, which we wanted to avoid, would then certainly have been inevitable. The blame for the blunder was not the less great because the circumstances under which it would have been made did not arise. The possible argument that I should have been justified in making serious objections—indeed, in case of need, in refusing to carry out the instructions—may be admissible in theory, in practice it falls to the ground. There would have been no time to urge objections, my refusal would have meant my recall, this again would have meant a rupture, and the rupture war.

A most deplorable mistake was made, however, in putting me in the position of having to account for the declaration of war on France by statements as to air attacks which the French would know at once were unfounded. However desirable it may have seemed, for military reasons, to turn the moment to account and accuse the French of having started hostilities, the step was too momentous to be taken without careful enquiry into the justification for it. Even if the alleged hostile acts had actually taken place, it would have been just as rash to attach the importance of a military offensive to them as it would have been unjustifiable in respect of the indiscretions of a few Hotspurs on our side. The French, as a rule so impulsive, were wise enough not to look on these isolated occurrences as a reason for declaring war, and to leave the odium of taking the offensive to us. Moreover, it may be a question whether the 'rejection of our proposal of neutrality, by which France announced that in a war between us and Russia she would stand by her ally, did not amply suffice to justify our breaking off relations with France as well. Whatever quarter may have been responsible for the mistake we made is guilty of having furnished our enemies with an extraordinarily effective handle for their " hate propaganda," and for accusing us of having unwarrantably attacked them. That my name should be coupled with a serious mistake, which gives the impression of having been an untruth, is the most painful recollection of my official life.

Having reached the German frontier on the way home, difficulties arose in the way of getting any farther. Our march westwards was in full swing, and the transport of troops made such claims on the line that no opportunity could

be given me of continuing my journey to Berlin.
There was nothing for it but to take the French
special train through to Berlin, assuming that it
would be brought back from there at once.
But in order to do this it was repeatedly necessary
to overcome the opposition of the officers in
command of the stations, who insisted on com-
mandeering the train and arresting the two French
guards. Finally, I was obliged to resort to the
drastic measure of putting on my military uniform
to ensure my being treated with respect. In
Berlin I even had to ask the Imperial Chancellor to intervene, to ensure the train being
given up and sent back.

On my arrival in Berlin I was immediately
given an opportunity of reporting my recent experiences and my impressions to the Kaiser and
the Chancellor. In doing so I expressed an
opinion that the war would be a long and
unspeakably serious struggle for existence. In
view of the immense superiority of our opponents
in resources of all kinds it appeared doubtful
whether we should be able to do more than
maintain our position and our honour, in spite
of our extraordinary efficiency. I referred at
some length to the fact, which had struck me,
that there was a tendency on our side to under-
rate the French military and national power of
attack and resistance, a view which had never
been encouraged by the Embassy reports. The
Kaiser's mood was grave, but absolutely calm
and confident. He was particularly pleased to
hear of the uniform enthusiasm and determination I had noted on my way back through

Germany. That was my last interview with him. My wish to be received in audience at the end of my term of office in Munich, which was at the same time the end of my diplomatic career, was not fulfilled.

I also found the Chancellor in a grave and confident frame of mind, but still agitated on account of England's declaration of war made the day before. He asked me if I thought an alliance with France would be possible. I replied that this seemed to me conceivable on two conditions : the first being our not carrying the war into French territory, and thereby compelling France's national strength to exert itself to the utmost. Whether it would be possible to observe this condition, from the military point of view, I could not say. The second condition would be that in case of our being victorious we should treat France very indulgently, above all where her honour was concerned ; we might perhaps even have to agree to a rectification of the frontier in Lorraine.

I had intended placing my services at the disposal of the military authorities, but this intention was not carried out, as the necessity arose of sending a higher diplomatic representative, well acquainted with Bavarian conditions, to Munich, to replace the Prussian Minister, who had been given an appointment at General Headquarters. The choice fell on me, and I willingly accepted the post. I remained in Munich as Minister for more than two years, until the moment came when the former Minister's duties at General Headquarters came to an end, and he returned to his post. With the end of my activity in the Bavarian capital, of which I have specially pleasant recollections, my diplomatic career came to an end, almost to the day, forty years after its commencement.

APPENDIX

THE CAUSE OF THE WAR

YEARS have gone by since the unhappy time when the language of peoples was the roar of the guns, and their paths torrents of blood. The weapons of bronze are idle, the outlines of a new life have been drawn, but still the spirit of peace has not descended on suffering humanity; the sea of hatred still surges, claiming its victims; violence stalks through the land, passions rage, the nations exhaust themselves in mutual accusations of having let loose the dogs of war. The minds of men are still too much under the influence of the tragedy to be capable of seeing clearly and forming an impartial opinion. Even with the most honest desire to examine the facts, there are obstacles in the way of distinguishing right from wrong, arising partly from our own, partly from the inability of others to see light and truth through the mist and darkness. Many attempts have been made to fix the blame, but none have yet led to friend and enemy recognising that all have made mistakes, all have done wrong. If another attempt is made here, it is less with the intention of intensifying the differences than with the idea of palliating our own and the mistakes of our enemies by considering them impartially. More is required to clear up the difficult question than a glance at what has recently occurred. We must look back at the distant past in order to see how it originated.

It must be evident even to the poorest observer that the obstinate refusal of the French people to recognise what had come to pass in 1871 as a permanent state of affairs was at the bottom of the unrest from which Europe suffered for far more than a generation. Embued with memories of former days, when France was the leading nation in Europe, the French could not reconcile themselves to having been pushed into the background by younger and stronger national forces, and having suffered painful loss of power, prestige, and territory. The people adhered persistently to the view that in depriving them of Alsace-Lorraine we had done them a great wrong, and that France's honour demanded its reparation. They were quite unable to understand the German point of view that, in an honest fight which had been forced upon us, we had won back the provinces taken from us by obvious force in days when we were helpless, and that it was indispensable to hold them as a guarantee against a renewal of the attacks from which we had so often suffered.

France had in fact acquired colonial possessions in Africa, Asia, and the Pacific, whose value far outweighed what she had lost, whilst we looked on benevolently, and by this means had soon risen once more to the level of a Great Power, had gained wealth and might, and opened up inexhaustible sources of strength; but this had not satisfied her injured pride and insulted honour; the wound inflicted by the Frankfurt peace had never healed. Time had somewhat allayed the pain, and silenced the passionate clamour for satisfaction, but the desire to win back what they had lost, and recover their former commanding greatness, had remained firmly rooted in the heart of the French people, and never for a moment ceased to be the centre of gravity of French policy, no matter what party might be in power. The "hopes" were sometimes relegated to the background, disguised under the cloak of silence, in accordance with Gambetta's teaching, but they were never extinguished. If they died down for a time, busy forces were still at work to keep the "sacred fire" burning and supply it with fuel, well knowing that the slightest breath of wind from without would revive it, and that the easily roused national feeling would burst into flames at the given moment.

And it was not only the lesser fanatical spirits, professional patriots, and journalistic hirelings, who kept up the fire, but also men who were shining lights in the intellectual world, in positions of the highest responsibility, leading statesmen, serious historians, past-masters of fiery eloquence. Professors of the Academy and school teachers were also pressed into the service of the *revanche* idea ; even the clergy threw themselves, in many cases with ardour, into the Nationalistic cause. There were military men of high standing who seldom spoke, but whose voices carried all the more weight, and revealed the ideas which prevailed at the War Office, ideas which aimed not only at recovering the "lost provinces" but at pushing forward the French frontiers to the Rhine. The "Rhine," so

Mollard of the General Staff wrote, "is not a German river at all, it is a frontier. It divides western Europe into two great districts, the French, extending from the ocean to the Rhine, and the German, extending from the Rhine to the Elbe. We have been, are, and shall remain, arch enemies." Even men who had no claim to greatness did not find it difficult to rouse and throw the nation into turmoil, when they declaimed against Germany, and raised the cry "Alsace-Lorraine." The era of Boulanger and Déroulède, which led to the verge of war, had shown this. "The heart of France was beating, all was in readiness, and all had absolute confidence in their leaders." It was proved by the Dreyfus affair, when passions were roused to such a pitch by the idea of treachery in the military intelligence service, of shameful betrayal to the German enemy, that an innocent man was condemned. There were, indeed, exceptional men such as Scheurer-Kestner and Zola, who had the courage to protest against this mistake, but they were not entirely successful; the light of truth did not penetrate into every heart; the mistaken belief that Germany was the enemy lying in wait behind the walls of the Vosges, hatching revenge, and longing to attack, still existed; the idea that Germany was the evil-doer, who, not satisfied with victory, set her heavy heel—*la botte ferrée de Bismarck*—on the neck of long-suffering France, was as strong as ever.

Comprehensible—nay, admirable—as this national spirit may have been from the purely human point of view, it was a matter of grave anxiety to politicians, a never-ending source of discomfort, perplexity, and danger of war. Lasting resentment at the humiliation of 1871, and the craving for retaliation, was the ever-potent force which drove French statesmen to seek compensation for France's seriously diminishing strength, owing to the decrease in the birth-rate, by calling in military assistance from the colonies, and forming close alliances with other Powers who were not well-disposed to Germany.   Imperial France had already strengthened her army by enlisting natives of Algeria ; the Republic opened up regions in the rest of North Africa, particularly in Senegal, which provided her with human material for the war far in excess of her expectations, both as regards quantity and quality. The persistent headway she made in those regions was in no small degree with the object of expanding those sources of supply.   But it was chiefly in alliances and agreements that France sought help, ostensibly for protection against German ambitions, in reality in order to carry out her idea of retaliation.   She turned first to Russia, making skilful use of existing possibilities.   The *rapprochement* began with the supply of French arms and French money— *nervus rerum*.   This was sufficient in itself to show its real object. When the alliance was finally concluded and had been proclaimed in Kronstadt, and celebrated in Moscow and Paris, the spirit in which the French welcomed the achievement was shown by the way in which the enthusiastic cry " *Vive l'Alsace-Lorraine!* " rang through the country.   In the course of years the alliance was deepened by special agreements as to the nature of military help on land and at sea, the last occasion being two years before the war, at the time of Poincaré's Ministry.

But for a long time the alliance with Russia did not fulfil the hopes of French eagerness for action ; Russian policy showed little inclination to make the Alsace-Lorraine question its own. France therefore looked about for further help that might be of use, overcame the old burning hatred for the sake of the cause, and concluded the *entente cordiale* with England after the Fashoda incident. Having regard to the fixed principles of English policy, the connection could not be an alliance, but it became a relationship of close friendship aimed against Germany, an aim which was perfectly evident more than once, and finally led, just as in the case of Russia, and almost simultaneously, to military agreements very much in the nature of an alliance. France had but one object in entering into all these agreements, and that was to prepare the ground for a final successful reckoning with Germany. If she had wanted peace, it would have been natural to seek it by keeping on tolerably good terms with us as neighbours ; we were willing, but France could not make up her mind to this unconditionally. She was, and remained, irreconcilable. In spite of various acts of courtesy and friendliness on our part, in spite of many and not always unsuccessful efforts to reach an understanding in individual spheres, to work with her in occasional international questions, indeed to bring about a general *rapprochement,* and in spite of calm intervals, the gulf remained open. It could only have been closed by the restoration of Alsace-Lorraine, or bridged over by our giving up part of it.

But in the course of time France also became our economic opponent, ever complaining more bitterly that we were driving her from her old markets in the world, thanks to the growth of our trade, our industry, and even our technical skill; that in spite of protective measures, bad feeling, and difficulties of all kinds, France and her colonies were increasingly flooded with German goods, German labour, and German industrial undertakings. French capitalism, a ruling power in France in spite of democratic rule and Socialistic theories, was disturbed at finding the conditions less easy than they had been, and alarmed at Germany's increasing share in the exploitation of France's natural resources, particularly of her mineral wealth. It consequently turned its strong influence on public opinion and on the political powers to account to arouse violent opposition to German economic expansion. Nationalism and Capitalism combined to drive the French nation into courses which must eventually lead to war with the assumed author of all evil, Germany.

It was not until quite recently, shortly before the outbreak of war, that the French way of thinking, sobered by the weight of the heavy burden of three years' military service, became more pacific, as the elections in the spring of 1914 showed. But it was too late: the march of the fate which had been courted could not be arrested; the rulers were caught in the more and more closely drawn network of alliances and agreements created by the policy formerly pursued ; the flames fanned by Nationalistic delusions burst out ; the people unanimously took up arms to defend their country and liberty against supposed German tyranny.

Things were otherwise with our neighbours in the East. An old friendship, based on brotherhood in arms, mutual services rendered, and close relations between the Courts, bound us to Russia. It was only when Russian nationalism—Pan-Slavism —became powerful, and pressed for fulfilment of the old dream of supremacy in Constantinople and the Dardanelles, and when this dream was dispelled at the Berlin Congress, that the friendship was first clouded, and the idea of a *rapprochement* to France was conceived. Thanks to Bismarck's statesmanship, however, friendly relations were maintained with Russia alongside of the alliance which had been concluded with Austria-Hungary, until the non-renewal of the Reinsurance Treaty dealt with them a fresh, and this time a serious, blow. The immediate result was the conclusion of the alliance with France, which involved an important change in the European situation to our disadvantage. Even then, by cultivating dynastic ties, we were still able to keep on good terms with Russia on the whole, so long as her immense strength sought and found a wide field for expansion in the Asiatic East. But when the Japanese War put an end to this activity, and the Empire was still further weakened by the Revolution, Russian policy once more aimed at a position in Europe, and the old goal, Constantinople.

There were obstacles in the way of this ; first of all Austria-Hungary, who was competing against

Russia for supremacy in the Balkans, and then Germany, who stood behind her ally, not egging her on, but protecting her in what she considered her own interests. Germany had also acquired a position in Turkey which she had to defend. "The road to Constantinople," it was said in Russia, "is via Vienna, the road to Vienna via Berlin." Thus differences arose which were intensified in proportion as the nationalistic spirit in Russia struggled, not without outside help, against the still influential German element of good old days, in proportion as complaints were made of German economic pressure, and closer *rapprochement* with the Western Powers was urged as a means of forcing Germany to keep more in the background. France was only too willing to provide Russia with the means of considerably increasing her armaments against the Central Powers, and England agreed to bury the Asiatic hatchet, and make common cause with Russia.

In this way forces hostile to us had come into being not only in the West but in the East, which were a menace to us, but must be far more menacing if they succeeded in getting a third Power, England, to throw in her lot with them entirely. Friendly relations had bound us to England, just as to Russia, for many years. They were based on blood relationship between the peoples and between their reigning Houses, on cultural resemblance, on similarity of religion, on the brotherhood in arms at Waterloo, as well as on the brisk and important trade between the two countries. It was in the latter sphere, the one in which the English are most sensitive, that the satisfactory relations were first prejudiced when we adopted the system of protective tariffs. In consequence of this change our economic life developed rapidly ; our trade, industry, and shipping increased to an extent which was disquieting to England. The disquietude became anxiety when our achievements enabled us to appear as England's successful rival in the markets of the world, when it seemed possible that we might overtake if not outstrip her commercially, when, having acquired important colonial possessions, we embarked on world-policy, and when, as the logical consequence of this, we finally proceeded to construct and arm a Navy whose strength and efficiency became a substantial and continual source of dissatisfaction, anxiety, and suspicion to the English people.

The absolute supremacy England had acquired in world-trade and on the high seas by centuries of toil with a definite aim, and which was secured by her possessions, her stations, and an extraordinarily powerful Navy, was vital to her position of world-power. This now seemed imperilled, and not only did England feel her trade routes all over the world menaced by our strength at sea, but also her position at home. The spectre of a German landing loomed large in the minds of people who had hitherto felt no anxiety, and the question arose whether it would not be advisable to oppose the expansion of the German Navy by force, before this became too dangerous an undertaking. Some talked of England's having already had to deal a blow to a Navy which she had reason to believe might

be employed to her injury, and in a responsible
quarter it was said that England " would strike
the first blow, before the other side had time to
read in the newspaper that war was declared."
As threats of this kind did not have the desired
effect, on the contrary, we quietly went on with
the German naval construction which had been
decided upon, Great Britain was obliged to maintain the great superiority of her Navy, and consequently to add very heavily to her financial burdens,
a state of affairs which was far from improving
the feeling towards Germany.

In addition to the anxiety felt as to Germany's increasing importance at sea, there was
anxiety as to the European balance of power.
According to this theory, England could not permit
any Power to acquire a ruling position on the
Continent.   From this point of view it was impossible for her to look on passively at a development which might enable Germany to overthrow
France, and even gain a footing on the coast from
whence she could hold a pistol at Great Britain's
head.   All these dangers could only be met by
the most strenuous military exertions and by making
stupendous financial sacrifices, or else by securing
outside help, either to intimidate or overthrow the
enemy.   *Germaniam esse delendam* became almost
a common saying in England.   Under these circumstances it is not surprising that after the dispute
with France over the Egyptian Sudan, which ended
in her favour, England should have concluded an
entente cordiale with her old enemy, and should,
later on, have approached Russia with a similar
object.

15

Although the agreements reached between France, Russia, and England did not, so far as England was concerned, constitute a formal alliance, their inherent spirit of antagonism to Germany, and the close co-operation of the new friends in all important international questions, gave them the same value, and it was an easy matter to stamp these friendly relations with the seal of alliance at the given moment. If a succession of others are added to those agreements directly aimed against Germany, the naval agreement with Spain and France, the efforts made by England, France, and Russia to secure Italy's friendship, the *rapprochement* between Russia and Rumania, the Anglo-Japanese alliance, and the agreements with Belgium, the result is a widespread network of alliances, friendships, and understandings, representing that which has been aptly described in Germany as " encirclement."

A situation has been created which the disadvantages of our geographical position, hemmed in as we were, made intolerable. It constituted our enemies sentinels over all we did or left undone, and enabled them to oppose any impulses of our exuberant national life that they found inconvenient, by any means they thought expedient, even by forcible means. They took good care to insist that there was no question of hostile action on their part, or of anything more than precautionary and defensive measures to avert dangers which were supposed to be threatened on our part, the German tendency to bully, the German craving for greatness, the German aspiration to supremacy in Europe and consequent world-supremacy.

German world - supremacy ! This accusation shows more than any other the inability of nations to understand one another. No sensible or responsible man in Germany had indulged in such bold flights of fancy, had thought of forcible expansion, or dreamt of conquering the world. Utterances, more remarkable for their sound than for their sense, did indeed fall here and there from boastful lips, a handful of noisy patriots did sometimes express ideas which might be said to reveal a craving for power, but that was not the voice of the German people, not the creed of leading men, not the aim of peaceable and well-meaning German policy.

What the German people and their leaders wanted was that their efforts and achievements should be recognised and rewarded ; they wanted to be allowed a fair share in the exploitation of the world's natural resources, and space in which to move and breathe freely, not at the expense of other nations, but in honest and peaceable co-operation with them. We did not want to drive any human being from his native soil, to force ourselves on anyone, or oppress any nation. It was only when the combustible material which had been heaped up round us burst into flames, and the blaze threw a lurid light on the magnitude of the danger, only then that we determined to break the ring which fenced us round, to burst the chains for ever. It was only in the heat of war, under pressure of our enemies' "will to destroy," that, in the flush of victory, thoughts took shape in the minds of the leaders, whose flight was ended by a sudden fall from the dizzy heights to which they had all too boldly soared.

It may be opportune to ask whether, to what extent, and how we could have counteracted this encirclement.

As far as France is concerned, to begin with, what we could gather almost daily in the course of years, from events, from the language of the Press, from political observation, and from the utterances of statesmen and politicians, left no doubt that we could never be on good terms with our western neighbour for any length of time, unless we agreed to give France's injured national honour full satisfaction by sacrificing what we had won in 1871. The celebrations before the statues in the town of Strasburg, the worship of Joan of Arc, the " Liberator," and the remarks hurled across the frontier by French Generals and Russian Grand Dukes, were further evidence of this, and it was established over and over again by the fundamentally irreconcilable drift of French policy. " *Rendez-nous l'Alsace-Lorraine, alors nous serons les meilleurs amis de la terre,*" was what M. Barthou had said to me with amazing candour a few months before the war.

That the payment of so high a price for a better understanding with the French was unthinkable, as far as we were concerned, need not be said. Every German looked on Alsace-Lorraine's forming a part of the Empire as an unalterable fact, for historical reasons, and because it was an agreed necessity. If time were left to do its healing work, there might well some day be a possibility, if not of altogether conciliating, at all events of appeasing, the French, either by an exchange, a frontier rectification, giving Alsace-

Lorraine full autonomy, or setting up a neutral zone. These were ideas which had occurred here and there to many French minds, and had they been carried into effect they might very well have bridged over the gulf. But the time had not come to discuss, let alone to act upon them. Although there were not a few who thought something of the kind practicable, the number who were of sufficient importance and had sufficient courage to champion these ideas in public was but small. No one responsible ever said a word openly which would have been an encouragement to friendly discussion. If anyone did so privately he was suspected of being a traitor, as the experience with Caillaux proves, reviled and persecuted, or assassinated like Jaurès. It was the same at the end as in the beginning : no Government could have remained in office for twenty-four hours which would have guaranteed Germany the possession of Alsace-Lorraine.

As things were, we could indeed come to an understanding with France as to individual questions, apart from the great bone of contention which divided us, and thus pave the way to further conciliation, but Alsace-Lorraine itself was always far too burning a question to be touched upon with our neighbours. Whether the healing hand of time would have accomplished the work of pacification more rapidly if much had been left undone which we did to keep the wound open, and rekindle the smouldering fire, is another question. It must be admitted that we did not always show tact. The state of affairs and the administration in Alsace-Lorraine were not calculated to make the process of severing the relations with France painless, and it cannot be denied that such incidents as the Kaiser's visit to Tangier, and our insistence on the Algeciras Conference, in spite of the Premier, M. Rouvier, having gone so far as to sacrifice M. Delcassé in his efforts to meet us, and, finally, the Agadir action, which was particularly offensive to French national feeling, had the effect of throwing cold water on all conciliatory movements in France, of imparting fresh strength to Nationalism, and influencing French policy to seek ever closer alliance with our enemies.

If we wanted our own views and conceptions to meet with sympathy and understanding, no nation, alongside of and with whom fate had decreed that we should live, needed more careful handling, a lighter touch, and more comprehension of their psychology than the French, with their excitable temperament and over-sensitiveness as regards their honour, particularly in view of their feeling towards us. A weak conciliatory attitude was certainly not desirable, still less a harsh peremptory manner. Our behaviour should have been outwardly dignified and chivalrous, whilst our policy was clear and resolute. "*Chez nous, on se salue de l'épée avant de se battre,*" was what a Minister said to me after the Agadir affair.

As regards Russia, our position was not one which afforded us much opportunity of diverting her policy into paths other than those on which she had embarked in her own vital interests. The fact of such a master of statecraft as Bismarck having been unable to prevent Russia's carrying away a feeling of annoyance from the Berlin Congress, which led to the idea of a *rapprochement* with France, is sufficient in itself to show that with the best will in the world it would have been quite beyond our power entirely to satisfy our eastern neighbour. Even at that time the position was such that we could not prejudice our cordial relations with England, who was then friendly towards us, for the sake of Russia, still less could we sacrifice the interests which made it advisable for us to stand by Austria-Hungary. All the same, we succeeded in keeping on fairly good terms with Russia, alongside of our alliance with Austria-Hungary, until the moment when, by not renewing the Reinsurance Treaty, we gave her reason to believe that we did not attach the same value to a formal bond of friendship with her as to one with the Habsburg Monarchy. Although our policy was at that time innocent of any unfriendly intentions towards our eastern neighbour, Russian suspicions were aroused, and the result was the conclusion of an alliance with France ! Russia thought it necessary to balance the loss on one side by a gain on the other, although the republican régime and democratic tendencies of the latter were less congenial to her than the German monarchical and Conservative alliance. At first Russia had no aggressive intentions ; on the contrary, the new relationship was so handled that the hopes the *revanche* party in France had set on the alliance were damped. Under the reign of the prudent Alexander III, Russia wanted peace, and had no inclination to plunge into adventures for the sake of a matter of so little concern to her as 'Alsace-Lorraine.

When the expansive energies of the Russian Empire found more scope under Nicholas II, and were directed eastwards, thus leading to war with Japan, we maintained an attitude which really showed more goodwill than that of her French ally. Russia owed us a debt of gratitude ; we were justified in expecting that she would turn to us with renewed cordiality after the war, and at all events cool off still more towards France, even if she did not abandon the alliance, from which she had gained very little. But the inexorable course of events, a stronger force than her own wishes, drove Russia into another and fresh direction. As a result of her defeat in the East and the revolution which succeeded it, she felt so weakened that she was no longer able to stand against the former hostility of her opponent in Asia, England, and felt obliged to throw herself into her arms. She needed relief in this direction all the more as, now that her Asiatic goal was beyond reach, she had to aim at Constantinople, which was nearer and more valuable. This goal was not attainable without agreement with England, and could not be approached by way of the Balkans without the help of Powers who did not, like Germany and Austria-Hungary, make the maintenance of the *status quo* in the Near East an irrevocably fixed item of their political programme. We could not prevent this readjustment of the European position without sacrificing our own vital interests, which compelled us to protect our Austro-Hungarian ally and Asiatic Turkey against Slav ambitions. For the same reasons we had soon afterwards to make common cause with the Danube Monarchy against the Russian Empire at the time of the Bosnian crisis, and to uphold it against the assaults and temptations from other quarters. It would certainly have been better if Baron Aehrenthal had not annexed Bosnia and Herzegovina in the high-handed and, to Russia, offensive manner in which he did this, without there being any urgent reason for it. It would also have been better if he had not broken the threads which had linked Austria-Hungary with Russia in the Murzteg Balkan agreement. We should then have been spared having had half to unravel, half to cut the knots in a way which caused bitterness in Russia, which strained the old friendship to breaking-point, and had no small share in creating the position which was responsible for the fatal catastrophe of 1914.

As far as our relations to England were concerned, matters were simpler. The old cordial relations could not have been maintained or restored while the English people had any cause for anxiety or animosity. In order to deprive them of this we should have had to call a halt in the rapid development of our trade, industry, and shipping, in our colonial activity, and in the measures we were taking to increase our defensive forces. That would almost have amounted to sacrificing ourselves as a nation. Many attempts were made to surmount the difficulties by understandings as to the colonies and spheres of influence, and particularly as to naval construction, in the hope of generally bringing about a better feeling between the two nations, and something really was achieved in this direction ; something valuable was achieved just before the war. But it seems doubtful whether these efforts would have led to a permanently satisfactory result. The vital conditions and necessities of the two countries would still have clashed. Even had we agreed to reduce our Navy very considerably, as we were persistently expected to do, the differences would not have been altogether at an end. The paths of the national energies on both sides, whose elementary force impelled them to seek an outlet in the world, had often crossed.

It must be admitted that, apart from the economic and military antagonism, other things, such as the loudly proclaimed enthusiasm of the German people for the Boers, and the Kruger telegram, had prejudiced the English people against us, but they were not what decided Great Britain's attitude towards us. On the other hand, it is certain that, in addition to the general and deeper reasons which decided her attitude, many a bombastic speech and significant act on our part, relating to the construction and activity of our Navy, contributed considerably to give prevalence to the saying " *Germaniam esse delendam* " on the other side of the North Sea. It may also be assumed that our relations, not only to England, but also to the other Powers, would have been better if we had not repeatedly protested at the Hague against the idea of limiting armaments, with a bluntness which did more honour to our straightforwardness than to our political judgment. Disarmament may have been a Utopian idea, but it would have been wiser to let this be recognised as the result of joint examination of the question than to have frustrated this by our refusal to take part in it, thereby incurring the odium of being the only ones unwilling to make any effort to diminish an intolerable burden and serious risks. Our attitude aroused a distrust which could not be dispelled by our later attempts, however honest, to reach an understanding with England over naval construction, and they were consequently unavailing.

Reflecting on the events which were immediately responsible for the war, apart from its deeper causes, it is obvious that, as often before, it was Serbia who wantonly played with the fire. The undermining work which had been carried on for years from Belgrade in the south-eastern portions of the Habsburg Monarchy, with the unmistakable object of revolutionising and detaching them, relying on the goodwill if not on express approval and encouragement from the great Slav Power, did not shrink from the most abominable methods, and had become so great a danger that, after repeated warnings, which had no effect, Austria-Hungary found it necessary to counteract these subversive activities with all her available energy. The Serajevo murder was startling evidence of the urgent necessity for crushing the rebellion at its centre.

In view of the enormity of the crime, and of the unsatisfactory experiences on former occasions, it can only too readily be understood that the Vienna Government now decided to demand, and if necessary exact, not only ample atonement, but absolutely secure guarantees against a continuance of the criminal agitation which was responsible for the misdeed. It was imperative to apply the remedy Count Achrenthal had summed up in the short saying : " Some day it will be necessary to take definite action in Belgrade," without further delay. There could be no doubt that this would bring Russia, the avowed protector of Serbia and instigator of the Balkan League, aimed against Austria-Hungary, on to the scene of action. At the same time it was a question how far Russia would go, whether the Tsar might not personally hesitate to exert his might in response to so criminal a battle-cry as the Serajevo murder, thus showing approval and support of the Serbian machinations. But if he were to do so, leading men in Vienna and Buda-Pesth thought there would be all the more reason for embarking on a life or death struggle, as evading it would not put a stop to the evil, and it would have to be fought out later on under circumstances of considerably increased difficulty, in the sense that Austria-Hungary would be further weakened and the enemy further strengthened. There was no longer any going back ; the domestic position of the Monarchy, as a result of the Slav subversive work, actively supported from outside, was such that it must inevitably fall to pieces, unless it pulled itself together now, and defeated the revolutionary forces for good and all.

All the same, long and serious consideration was given to the question of the amount of satisfaction and security to be demanded of Serbia, and the tone to be adopted in making the demands. Should it be made easy for Serbia to submit and turn over a new leaf, should harsh conditions be imposed which would be a salutary humiliation, or would it be better to act in such a way as necessarily to bring about a rupture which would leave the

Monarchy free to put a forcible end to the Slav peril? The objection to the first was that it would not root out the growing evil; to the second, that it might lead to tedious discussions and interference from outside; to the last, that it might develop into a struggle involving heavy sacrifices, and that no one could foretell how far it might extend. Finally, after some hesitation, it was decided that the demands should be so far-reaching and so peremptory, that Serbia must either humbly submit to the will of the Habsburg Monarchy, thus prejudicing her sovereignty and abandoning her political aims and her secret connections with the Russian Empire, or, by not accepting all the conditions, refuse to submit. Consequently, the substance and form of the Note to the Belgrade Government were as harsh as it was possible to make them. They left no loophole for evading or haggling over the demands. But the Vienna Government made one important reservation: under no circumstances was the action against Serbia to aim at annexation, or go beyond exacting reparation.

In view of the close alliance between us, it need not be said that the Vienna Government did not take such a grave step without coming to an understanding and discussing its importance with us, and making sure of our approval and support. We recognised that it was not a question of an unprovoked attack, with the object of annexation, but of reparation and self-defence, of striking at the root of dangers which not only seriously threatened the existence of our ally, but indirectly our own; consequently we thought it right not to refuse the consent and support asked. If these dangers became still more menacing, and the Austro-Hungarian Monarchy were to fall to pieces through the undermining influence and attacks of united Slavdom, what would remain of it would not at the best be strong enough to be valuable to us as an ally. We should then stand alone at the mercy of hostile Powers infinitely superior to us in strength, as we could no longer depend on Italy.

We fully realised that our ally's was a bold venture. There was always the possibility that Russia might in some way come to the rescue of her hard-pressed protégé. But although Russia was no longer in the same position as at the time of the Bosnian crisis, on the contrary, she was well armed and ready for action, and would not be willing to put up with a fresh diplomatic defeat, still we were justified in assuming that she would be cautious, in view of the criminal origin of the conflict. It was hardly conceivable that so definitely monarchical an Empire would openly support a country which traced the lines of its destiny in the blood of its own and other sacrosanct heads. Should anything so unconceivable happen, the hostile strength would be so great, the position so serious, that we could only hope to avert the dangers by facing them resolutely with united forces.

Our course was consequently marked out: to state our intention of loyally adhering to our alliance, avert outside interference, and prevent disastrous intervention. We lost no time in taking the first step by announcing to the Powers

that, under the circumstances, we could not but
approve of our ally's procedure, but that we
were not interfering in any way in the disputes, and in order to avoid more serious complications we could only strongly advise their
adopting the same attitude. Although this well-
intentioned proposal to localise the conflict was
entitled to appreciation, as having made the
position perfectly clear from the start, and indicated a practicable way in which to maintain
European peace, the result was not satisfactory.
The idea of localisation was, indeed, agreed to
in London, and temporarily in Paris too, but
all the same our communication roused suspicion
and was misunderstood. Paris was instantly ready,
to regard it as proof of a cleverly precon-
certed arrangement between us and Vienna to
disturb the peace of Europe, and to accept it
less as a counsel of peace than a harbinger of
war. In St. Petersburg it was checkmated by
the announcement that Russia would not be able
to stand aside, a hint which was strongly underlined by immediate military preparations. Besides this, the French and Russian authorities had
already decided to interfere. This brought about
the very thing we had tried to prevent. Instead
of being confined to the narrow limits of the
two States concerned, the conflict spread to the
extensive and dangerous area of the great European
differences. Russia did not scruple to throw
the weight of her prestige and power into the
scale in favour of a criminal policy, and act as
Serbia's protector, without even condescending to
notice the assurance the Vienna Government had

given at once, that they were not aiming at anything more than reparation and guarantees.

England, indeed, tried to intervene and pacify, but without the success which had attended her former efforts. Sir Edward Grey ought, after all, to have realised that it would be difficult to carry out his proposal that Powers who were not concerned should hold conferences and make representations, if only because it contravened the principle of avoiding outside interference on which we had laid stress. After the failure of our "localisation proposal," and in view of Russia's menacing attitude, we considered St. Petersburg the centre where further efforts to maintain peace should be made, and later events proved that we were right. But our representation to this effect met with no response. France in particular evaded, if she did not actually refuse the request. We, on the other hand, were not only willing, but did our utmost to bring about a conference between Vienna and St. Petersburg, even going so far as to exert strong pressure on our ally, in our sincere desire to avert the worst, and our efforts met with some success. But they were frustrated, first by the Vienna Government's hesitation, and then by Russia's obstinacy, which was considerably strengthened by the certainty that England would intervene, and was already demonstrated by the mobilisation against Austria-Hungary.

And Russia was not satisfied with this. On the contrary, in spite of the fact that we were still trying to mediate, and that we were consequently on the road to a peaceable solution, in

spite of our most urgent entreaty to her not
to let loose a European war, she took the fatal
step of mobilising against us; a threat and a
challenge to which we were compelled to reply,
first by an ultimatum, and, when that failed, by
mobilising and declaring war. This brought matters
to such a pass that a fresh English proposal
that military measures should be suspended all
round had no more chance of success than the
Tsar's suggestion to appeal to arbitration.   As
France did not agree to our proposal of neutrality,
and, on the contrary, completed the extensive
military preparations she had already made by
formally mobilising and assembling her Army,
we were obliged to declare war on her too,
whilst England made our invasion of Belgium a
reason for breaking off relations with us.

In considering the events of these critical July
days, special mention must be made of an unfortunate circumstance ; that is, Austria-Hungary's
having been insufficiently prepared and having
delayed her military measures. Had the Monarchy
been in a position to reply to the rejection of
her ultimatum by invading Serbia at once and
occupying Belgrade, the prospects of limiting
the conflict would probably have been better ;
the prestige of the Habsburg Monarchy would
have been upheld, the Serbs and their Russian
supporters would have been shown that Austria-
Hungary was both determined and able to preserve her dignity and her existence, and Count
Berchtold would not have been obliged to make
the reservation, in accepting the Grey proposal
of mediation, that the military action against

Serbia must take its course. It was this reservation which aroused suspicion, and was largely responsible for its no longer being possible to reach an understanding as to limiting the conflict.

The deeper causes of the war lay in the far distant past, as a glance at history will show. They had their origin in those national movements, corresponding to the love of possessions and power, instinctive in human nature, which have taken the form of Imperialism, Nationalism, Pan-Slavism, Militarism, and Capitalism', according to the character and lot of the peoples, and the influences on their minds, all of which have been more or less cursed with a tendency to seek the welfare of individuals and nations by forcible means. Far-seeing people recognised betimes and correctly that, once they were freed from the fetters that bound them, these antagonisic movements threatened to come into collision with frightful force. Efforts were made to avert the catastrophe, and were partially successful, but in the long run they were unavailing, either because the forces which swept away the barriers were stronger than those setting them up, or because the right ways of averting the evil were not taken. That is where all the Powers drawn into the disputes, including Germany, were more or less seriously mistaken.

Russia was undoubtedly the Power most to blame. The Russian Empire wanted and brought about the war because it needed it. War appeared to the ruling upper class the only way out of the danger of internal complications ; to the

Neo-Slavs it held out a prospect of their schemes being carried into effect; the Social Revolutionaries hoped it would bring about the downfall of Tsarism. Russia was fully prepared and in fighting trim, thanks to French encouragement and ample help, long before the Serajevo "chance" presented itself. "There is no such thing as chance, and that which seems to us blind chance is just what has the deepest sources." In this case they were Russian, genuinely Russian sources, in spite of the German-sounding label, "Hartwig." This man, the soul of the Russo-Serbian machinations against Austria-Hungary, did not survive his fatal work, but it survived him, to the misfortune of his country and of the world. And after the first outbreak of the fire she herself had laid, official Russia's attitude was hardly less reprehensible : she opposed all efforts to extinguish it, presumptuously defended political immorality, and unsheathed the sword.

France aided and abetted Russia. For years past weapons had been forged without intermission with which to fight us, gold and bronze and spiritual weapons. In addition to the alliance, agreements were carefully drafted with a view to attacks on land and sea, and shortly before the war England was urged to enter into similar agreements. In the critical summer days after the Serajevo misdeed no attempt was made to allay the dangers ; on the contrary, repeated explicit assurances of help were given. No arguments, however skilful, no assertions, however vehement, that France did her utmost to prevent the war, can alter the fact that at the time of the greatest tension the French rulers did nothing to restrain their ally from her disastrous action. In spite of our urgent request, not a word was said in St. Petersburg against mobilisation ; on the contrary, it was encouraged by the information that England's support might be relied upon. In addition to that, France made hasty and extensive military preparations, rejected our proposal of neutrality, and, over and above all, overwhelmed us with unreasonable suspicions and accusations, with the object of making it appear that we had intrigued to bring about the war, had borne false witness in defence of our ally, had made hypocritical proposals and stood obstinately in the way of mediation, had forcibly got the better of the French pacific moderation, and finally, being hard up for an excuse for a rupture with France, had been obliged to try to find one, as at Ems, in the absurd suggestion that the Ambassador had been personally insulted.

It was the same with England. Plans were carefully laid there which could only have an aggressive object. Military agreements were concluded with France and Belgium, and, at the last moment, with Russia too. During the critical days no inclination was shown to work for the maintenance of peace in St. Petersburg, where alone efforts in that direction could have been effective. On the contrary, simultaneously with a succession of proposals of mediation, Russia was promised help.

Austria-Hungary's mistakes are patent. Instead of trying to reach an understanding with her rival for supremacy in the Balkans, sabre-rattling (more with our sabre than her own), both during the annexation crisis and again during the Sera-jevo crisis, inherent incompetence, overrating her own strength, underrating that of her opponents, an ultimatum so harsh as to overshoot the mark and affect Russia as well as Serbia, lack both of discernment, candour, and backbone.

As far as Germany is concerned, her enemies abroad, and the opponents at home of her quondam rulers, all accuse her of having had more faith in might than right, of having shown an arrogant and boastful military spirit, and acted and spoken offensively in the days before the war. Not without reason, although there can hardly be any doubt that in these respects our enemies were no less to blame. As regards the period when war broke out, prominence is given to three important points : our support of the ultimatum to Serbia, the declaration of war on Russia, and our invasion of Belgium. The German Govern-ment never has denied, and never could deny, her joint responsibility for the Note to Serbia. It was admitted in the first communication to the Powers, in which we stated that we entirely approved of the step taken by our ally, and gave our reasons. This detracts from the im-portance of the much-discussed and hotly dis-puted question whether we were aware of the exact text of the ultimatum which was eventually drafted in Vienna, or not. This has always been denied by the Government, and the fallacy of the contention that we did know of it is supported by the fact that Austria-Hungary's sovereignty entitled her to choose her own methods of carrying out her decisions.

It is true that if Germany were to be considered jointly to blame because she was jointly responsible, a view which does not seem warranted, seeing the weighty reasons she had for supporting her hard-pressed ally, and that she firmly believed the Viennese intended acting with moderation, her ignorance of the actual wording of the Note would not make her the less to blame. Some means could surely have been found of having a good look at our ally's arrow before it was shot. The Vienna Government's omission to give us any opportunity of doing so was most unfortunate. But at all events the German Government can claim the credit of having acted straightforwardly, and made strenuous efforts to localise the conflict, of having counselled and finally strongly urged moderation in Vienna

It is more difficult to decide the question whether we could have avoided replying to the Russian mobilisation by an immediate ultimatum, and by declaring war when the ultimatum proved unavailing. Less blunt and precipitate action on our part would certainly have given both the English proposal that military measures should be suspended all round, and the conversations between Vienna and St. Petersburg, a better chance of success. On the other hand, looking at the matter impartially, it must be remembered that for Germany to have meekly put up with the extremely menacing steps taken by Russia, and restricted her military preparations to exactly the same limits, would have implied a considerable amount of confidence that Russia would not go a hair's breadth beyond mobilisation. After the melancholy experience we had just had of Russian pacific assurances, we could not feel that degree of confidence, even in the Tsar's word. Events had proved that our leaders were only too justified in believing that the mobilisation of Russia's whole Army and Navy was a direct menace of such a serious nature that the steps must be taken without a moment's delay which would still be inevitable even if we postponed them, and would then be infinitely more difficult. The only weapon those who guided our destiny could oppose to the Russian superiority was greater rapidity of action. The fatal course of events had become the more inevitable in consequence of the fact that the moment Russia mobilised, the control necessarily passed automatically from diplomatic into military hands.

Things were otherwise as regards the invasion of Belgium. The decision to take this step was the result of the strategical view that a flank attack on the weaker side of the French position must be made as rapidly as possible, regardless of political considerations, and turned to account for a destructive blow. After the success of our undertaking in the West, our full strength was to have been thrown against the Russian forces, which would in the meantime have been slowly deployed. The calculation turned out to have been mistaken; the Russians were in position quicker, and in greater strength, than could have been foreseen. On the other side, the French Army was driven back a considerable distance at first, but was able not only to make a stand, but to carry out a powerful counter-offensive, thanks partly to its own strength and partly to English help. These first experiences of the war convinced many that it would have been wiser to take up a defensive position against France in the first instance, and make the greater effort on the east front. This would also have accorded with a correct psychological estimate of the French people, who would not readily have decided on a costly offensive against our strong front for the sake of a pre-eminently Russian cause, but whose patriotic enthusiasm and self-sacrificing devotion were roused to a pitch which exceeded all expectations against the enemy in their own country.

The fact of most importance, however, was that our advance into Belgium was responsible for England's decision to intervene, and to develop a strength which overstepped the apparently impassable limits fixed by her traditional principles. But the violence done to Belgium was not only a strategical and political error, it was also a breach of international law, as the competent authorities had to admit from the first. Neither the appeal to necessity nor the fact, which subsequently came to light, that Belgium had entered into relations with the Entente Powers with a view to a German invasion, could alter this. It was both wrong and dishonourable, it exposed us to the contempt of the world, and furnished our enemies with weapons with which they fought us no less effectively than by force of arms. The hardships of the campaign and of the occupation did all and more than was required to lash our enemies' hatred into fury. It may be quite correct, from a military point of view, to carry the horrors of war successfully into the enemy's country, but crushing a weak country, protected by sacred treaties, is a crime against which the world's conscience revolts, and for which it demands reparation. Germany will have to bear the burden of this reparation for a generation to come.

The truth is that Germany is not free from blame, but neither is she to blame in the sense and to the extent of which she is accused. She made mistakes, and did wrong, but not so much from lack of " will to peace " as from lack of safe guidance through the complexities of high policy. Like all the Powers, she reckoned with the possibility of warlike developments, and armed accordingly, but she did not seek the Great War, did not work deliberately for it, did not, as her opponents say, " wish for the war." The " will for war " only took possession of the people when the Janus gateway was opened by others, when Germany was forced to recognise that she must fight for her existence. The emergency compelled her to take rapid military action ; she was the apparent but not the real aggressor. The war did not originate in the brain of an individual statesman, was not caused by what one nation did or left undone ; it was the disastrous result of antagonisms between the Powers, engendered by elementary national impulses, and of there being no master mind to settle them peaceably.

INDEX

Printed in Great Britain by
UNWIN BROTHERS, LIMITED
LONDON AND WOKING

My Memoirs

By PRINCE LUDWIG WINDISCHGRAETZ

Demy 8vo.   TRANSLATED BY CONSTANCE VESEY   16s. *net.*

"We have seen no more vivid and dramatic account of the last stage of Hapsburg rule than that which Prince Ludwig Windischgraetz has written "—*Spectator.*

The Master Spinner

A BIOGRAPHY OF SIR SWIRE SMITH

By KEIGHLEY SNOWDEN

Demy 8vo.   *With Frontispiece*   16s *net*

"A biography, which for intimacy of treatment, combined with unusual restraint and good taste, can scarce have had its equal of recent years "—*Westminster Gazette.*

"One of the most delightful biographies I have ever read."— SIR W. ROBERTSON NICOL, in *British Weekly*

Seventy Years among Savages

By One of Them

Demy 8vo.   HENRY S. SALT   12s 6d *net.*

"Most entertaining . . . If Mr. Salt rides his fads hard, at least he shows a sense of humour and a wide acquaintance with people worth knowing."—*Westminster Gazette.*

"Whatever he is . . he is not a bore , the personal anecdotes are many and diverting. His book ought to be read for its serious purpose as well as for its lighter parts."—*Times Literary Supplement*

Joseph Gundry Alexander

Cr. 8vo.   By HORACE G. ALEXANDER   7s. 6d. *net*

"This concise memoir of a singular, full and active life fully justifies itself. . . . So telling a picture of a life of unconquerable devotion "— *Times.*

LONDON   GEORGE ALLEN & UNWIN LIMITED
RUSKIN HOUSE, 40 MUSEUM STREET, W.C. 1